Billy Graham

A Tribute: Classic Sermons of Billy Graham

By Patrick Doucette

***

Published by Kindle

Billy Graham: A Tribute

Classic Sermons of Billy Graham

By Patrick Doucette

Table of Contents

Preface

The date was June of 1995 and I had signed up to be an usher for the coming Billy Graham crusade. It was being held in my then hometown of Toronto, Ontario, Canada. The stadium was called the Skydome; a massive structure that could hold 70,000 people if you included the space on the field for extra seating. I was a young student and I was excited about the prospect of helping out in a such a significant event.

A flyer from the Billy Graham Crusade the author attended.

Four nights of preaching and each and every night, the stadium was full to capacity; many came late and unfortunately were not able to get in and access the general open seating. Before each evening, hundreds of people came early and anxiously pressed against the main glass doors waiting to get in. I had to open the doors just enough for the support workers to get in so they could start the preparations for the crowd.

Each time I would open the door just a fraction, a crush of people thought the doors were opening and would try and push forward. One woman even fainted and at times I was fearful there would be a stampede of sorts or that someone might get seriously injured. I was relieved when I could finally open the doors fully to let the crowd enter and take their seats.

Never before had so many Christians gathered together at one time in the city. As the people came in and were seated; a man on the stage stepped to the microphone and announced the stadium itself had never been filled with that many people before. Every possible square foot of space in the stands and on the open field had been filled with seats.

As the people filled the stadium, I looked out from the upper level over the mass of humanity that had gathered. Every Christian denomination was there, Catholics, Protestants, you name it; you could see people from every culture and race you could name. They had strung up speakers that translated the service into different languages so that people could understand what was being said; dozens of languages. And of course many non-Christians had been invited to hear the Gospel message as presented by Dr. Graham. I felt a powerful kinship with the people around me. I couldn't help wonder if a gathering of this sort would be any different had Jesus Himself been scheduled to appear; I imagined it would simply be similar but on a larger scale. The people who came to this event were hungry to have 'Peace with God'; they wanted to hear the Good News once more and to know that their sins could be forgiven.

The experience of those four days affected me deeply for a long time afterwards and perhaps I am still affected by having gone through that glorious experience. It gave me a renewed sympathy for and an association with the deep desires of the masses of humanity that seek God at a fundamental level. The simplicity and the honesty of the message had a special beauty.

At the end of one of the evenings, I remember that they announced Dr. Graham was leaving the stadium, that his car had arrived to take him to his Hotel. I peered over a cement barrier out onto a lower platform and sure enough, I saw him leaving out a rear entrance. What a strange coincidence I was positioned right where he was leaving. I stood in silence for a moment and then I called out "Dr. Graham" hoping he would wave. He did not wave but gave a kindly smile and I was thinking that perhaps he was out of earshot; I called out once more, "God Bless You" and with that he was gone; whisked away from the loud crush of the crowds to somewhere that was no doubt a safer, quieter location.

My heart was checked for looking too much towards "the man" and not enough towards the Savior but then I was also a bit sad to see how much this servant of the Gospel was needed and depended upon by so many diverse people. At that time Billy Graham was already seventy-seven years old and you could see that the years and the natural aging process had taken their toll; he moved slow; his hair was completely white and he stooped as he walked. This was a man that did not 'retire' at age sixty-five. He kept going in service to God, in service to the hundreds and thousands of Christian churches that depended on him and in service to the millions of fellow human beings that he loved and cared for so much.

~ Patrick Doucette

Introduction

Billy Graham was and is arguably one the most respected and well known preachers in America of the twenty-first century. Yes, he does have his detractors; as does anyone who tries to spread the Good News of the Gospel. But in general he has been admired and honored by millions of people throughout the world for his consistent and straightforward message of hope.

On November 7th, 1918, William Franklin Graham Jr. was born in Charlotte, North Carolina. He grew up on the family farm and at the age of sixteen made the decision to follow Christ after attending revival meetings conducted by Mordecai Ham. College was difficult for Billy Graham and he went from Bob Jones College to Florida Bible Institute and then finally graduated from Wheaton College.

He married his beloved wife Ruth Bell in 1943 and they were devoted to each other until her death in 2007 after sixty four years of marriage.

Billy Graham began preaching and serving as a Pastor as early as during his time in College and quickly became a leader; even becoming President of Northwestern Bible College at the age of 30. His was chosen for a major appointment to Christian service when he was selected as the full time evangelist for the newly formed Youth for Christ International in 1946.

From the start of his preaching ministry, Graham liked to conduct revival meetings and tent meetings similar to what he experienced as an audience member in his youth. He took the format to a new level by conducting 'crusades' which would last for weeks in a particular city; often they would include services every night of the week. Some say that he received support early on from the beneficial coverage of newspapers that were influenced by William Randolph Hearst. However, that would only account for a small fraction of his popularity as the newspapers controlled by Hearst would not explain his successful acceptance in countries all over the world including Russia and countries in Eastern Europe.

The services that Bill Graham conducted in cities all over the world will be a powerful memory for many; indeed that is where most people have actually seen him in person. Even though he was well known in the media as a friend to Presidents and a voice for peace, it is from his preaching messages that most will have a direct connection. It is with that memory in mind that this collection of sermons is presented to the reader; it is this legacy that still burns brightly in the hearts of those who heeded his message; those who said, "yes" to his invitation and exhortation to be 'born again'.

When Bill Graham preached, he almost always focused on scriptures from the New Testament. He related the stories of Nicodemus or Zaccheus or Lazarus; and he always spoke in such a way you could not help feel your faith being strengthened; it almost seemed like 'he was there'; it was as if he was present in the first century with Christ and was relating the scriptures from first hand memory- such was his fervor; such was his   .

powerful and inspired delivery of the good news of the

Gospel.

My earnest hope is that these sermon

transcriptions will inspire and encourage you while

simultaneously bringing honor to a great Christian

leader and tireless worker in God's Kingdom and also

and most importantly that they will bring glory to God

and His Son Jesus Christ, the author and finisher of our

faith.

May God Richly Bless You in All Things ~ Patrick

Doucette

Chapter 1 - Is There An Answer?

Thursday, October 6th, 1955 The Empire Club, Toronto , Ontario, CANADA

Mr. Chairman, gentlemen, members of The Empire Club, and friends who are gathered here today, it is a great delight and privilege for me to be here. I am also grateful for the very generous remarks that have been made by your President, and I am reminded of an incident that happened to the Archbishop of Canterbury some years ago. He was scheduled to visit an orphanage. In preparing for the occasion, the head of the orphanage gathered all the children together and said, "Now, when the Archbishop comes, there is a certain protocol you must observe. The Archbishop of Canterbury is always addressed as either "My Lord" or "Your Grace", and that is the way you are to address him if he stops and talks to any one of you."

So the Archbishop came. When he stopped in front of one little boy, he asked, "Son, how old are you?"

The little boy, frightened, looked up and answered, "My God, I am ten."

Now after the introduction that I have had today and the statistics that have been quoted, I am not sure exactly what you think of me, but we have been looking forward to coming.

I heard a story the other day about a Texan who was playing jokes on another Texan-and when two Texans play jokes on each other, they are really jokes, for they carry to some extremes. It seems that this man had been doped by his friends-he had been given some sort of drug that put him to sleep. They had prepared a grave for him out in the cemetery; and so they put him in the coffin, carried him out to the cemetery and buried him in this grave-but they didn't cover it. The next morning when he awoke, he looked all around and saw that he was lying in a coffin. He looked up at the clear blue sky, then stood up in the grave and looked around at the other tombstones. All of a sudden he gave a shout: "Hallelujah! This is the resurrection morning, and a Texan is the first one up."

I am certain that The Empire Club has a certain amount of pride in the Commonwealth of Nations, and more particularly in the Commonwealth of Canada. It has been my privilege to be in many parts of the British Empire and recently to spend a great deal of time in the British Isles and to make many friends there.

Most of us are aware, I think, that not only Great Britain but also the United States and the entire world are battling, as one United Nations delegate recently said, for our very survival. Economically, morally, politically, religiously and otherwise, we are battling against forces of materialism and humanism and communism that are beating at our gates from without and infiltrating from within. We are living in a period of world history that could either mean the beginning of a new day in history in which all mankind could be lifted to new economic levels and a new standard of living or we could be living in a day in which the entire world could be swept into destruction.

A German scientist recently said in Germany that it is now possible to depopulate the entire earth. That seems strange: that we must be afraid of weapons today. With the advance of science, with the lifting of economic conditions, with the parts of the world that have been illiterate learning to read and write and having advantages of educational, medical and social help that they have not had before, it seems strange that ours should be an age of fear.

Many people are asking, Why? They are asking: What is the solution to our many problems? Which way can we turn? Is there an answer?

Many people feel there is an answer in the United Nations. Others feel there is an answer in economic help to the under-privileged and in the Four Point Programme that President Truman outlined a few years ago. There are many people today with various answers.

Everybody is having his say. And now, today, I want to have a say. I want to go back two thousand years to find the answer to the dilemmas and the problems that we face. The United States and Canada were founded by Godfearing men. Whether their faith was Catholic or Protestant they came to these shores believing in God. They had a Bible in their hand. They put into the very foundation of our government "In God We Trust." They believed in Almighty God. They had a strong faith in religious liberty and a strong faith in the Almighty. They believed in God and the Bible. They made the Bible the very basis of our way of life and of our government and of our laws.

But a few years ago we decided that we no longer needed this faith, we no longer needed the Bible, we no longer needed God; and about the turn of the century we saw something happen. We began to feel that in the scientific, economic and industrial advances we had made that somehow science and religion could not be brought together and that religion was something belonging to the archaic past, that it was a group of myths, something to be done away with-and we almost agreed with Lenin when he said it was the opiate of the people.

So we discarded religion. Particularly in intellectual circles, we discarded the supernaturalistic concept: we said we no longer believed in God, we no longer believed in the Bible. So we substituted other things: Reason, Rationalism, Mind Culture, Science Worship, Freudianism, Naturalism, Humanism, Behaviourism, Positivism, Materialism - all the other isms we substituted for religion.

As a result, what happened? We developed our minds and neglected our souls. We forgot that we are more than just bodies with animal passions, animal lusts and animal desires. Oh, yes, we have bodies with eyes and ears and nose and hands and feet. Every one has a body with certain appetites that need satisfying: hunger, sex, thirst, the desire to be with each other, - the herd instinct - all of these things are passions and desires and appetites of the body. So we set about to satisfy our bodies. Our minds also have certain desires to acquire knowledge, so we set about to fill our minds with knowledge. But we neglected a third, a very important part of the human anatomy: the soul. We starved our souls, spiritually, and our souls began to shrivel. We forgot that we had been created in the image of God and that we had living souls that also had appetites. These appetites could only be satisfied by a faith and a communion with God.

We made money; we acquired knowledge; we developed scientifically, until one day we found ourselves with hydrogen bombs in our hands without the ability to control them, and until Sir Winston Churchill said: "We have progressed scientifically and materially, but we have lagged far behind morally, and now our problems have gone beyond us." When Sir Winston asked on the floor of the House of Commons: "Is there an answer?" he sat down without answering the question, because I think even the world's greatest statesman wasn't sure that there was an answer.

We faced a dilemma: the problem of full heads but empty souls. We had departed from the idea of God. We had reared a whole generation by telling them we even doubted that there was a God. Certainly we didn't believe in accepting Him, following Him and serving Him; and morals, instead of being absolute, became relative. Instead of saying that certain things are right and certain things are wrong, and making it clearly white and black, we made it all a dull gray. We said that you could lie and cheat and be dishonest-and we called it "good business."

So our moral standard began to break down, and we began to see the symptoms of this moral breakdown in our society: it broke out into juvenile delinquency, racial hatreds, prejudice and bigotry. All the vast problems that we face today have come about because we have starved the souls of men. Men desire something more than bread to eat, and we remember the words of one of long ago who said: "Man shall not live by bread alone." We need more than bread, we need more than gadgets, ice boxes, automobiles and airplanes.

Why would a beautiful young movie star in Hollywood, at the age of twenty-nine, with a million dollars in the bank, a beautiful face, her name known all over the world, try to commit suicide?

Why would a Texas millionaire, with a hundred million dollars in oil reserves, bow his head the other day and say, "I am the most miserable man in Texas"?

I ask some of you here today . . . you have prestige, you have money; but you haven't found inward peace and happiness and security in your own life-why? You have everything to make a person happy, according to the textbooks, but you haven't found the inward peace you are looking for. Why? Because you have forgotten one thing: you have forgotten you are also a soul created in the image of Almighty God, and that soul, as Saint Augustine said long ago, is restless until it rests in God.

So we produced an age of frustration. Everybody is frustrated. There is nervous tension. I think if historians write up this age, they will call it the Vitamin Capsule Age. We are taking aspirin by the million. In the United States we are taking over three million sleeping tablets every month to go to sleep at night, and then we are taking dexedrine to wake us up in the morning. We have every type of tablet you can possibly think of.

This is an age of selfishness, an age of fear. Look at the titles of the best sellers: The Decline of the West, The Decay and Restoration of Civilization, Civilization on Trial, The End of Our Time, The Crisis of Our Age, The Crisis of Civilization, The Annihilation of Man, The Abolition of Man.

Professor Albert Webber has said: "We are now at the end of history, and we know it."

William Voght, in his Road to Survival, says: "The day of judgment is at hand."

Pessimistic titles! We missed it somewhere. Where did we miss it? We have accepted alternatives to religion and all around us we view the ruins of the secular state offered to humanity as a substitute for religion.

Five years ago, before Mr. Eisenhower's inauguration as President, I had the privilege of being invited to the Commodore Hotel in New York City. I came in, and there sat the man who was to be President of the United States. He got up and greeted me and then went to the window for a full minute. When he turned around, he said: "Billy, do you know why I believe I have been elected President?"

I said, "I think I know several reasons, Sir."

He said: "I think one of them is to help lead America in a religious revival which we must have."

Some time ago it was my privilege to spend forty minutes alone with Sir Winston Churchill when he was Prime Minister at his office at Number 10 Downing Street. In the midst of that conversation he made this statement: "We must have a religious renaissance."

Arnold Toynbee, the great British historian, has said that only a revival of Christianity can save us.

If this is true - and the President has said it, the Prime Minister has said it, the Historian has said it, the scientists are saying it, then I say to you today that you and I, as ordinary citizens, had better be about it! It is the only way out of our dilemma. If the only way for the survival of our boys and girls, the next generation, is a religious revival, we had better be about it in every way we can.

But there is another reason, and that is that you and I have everlasting souls that are accountable to Almighty God. If you are to find peace for the rest of the days of your life, and peace in those last moments and in that hour when you shall stand before your Maker, you had better do something about it!

There was a Man-He wasn't an ordinary man, He was different from any man who ever lived-who came along two thousand years ago and said: "I have an answer." He gave to us in the Sermon on the Mount the greatest moral and social document the world has ever known, but we have never been able to live up to it. Oh, we have tried, but we have failed Why? Because we find no strength within ourselves to live up to it. Everyone has tried to live up to the Sermon on the Mount at some period in his life, but failed. You have no strength, you are not man enough, because when you want to do good, you do bad, and there is something that seems to pull you down all the time and makes you do the things you really don't want to do.

What is it? What is the answer? We forgot one thing this Man said. He was born a man, but He was the God-Man, walking in human flesh; and He said this: "Ye must be born again." What did He mean by this? That is a strange statement. He said it to an educated man, to an intellectual. He said it to a great leader. He said to Nicodemus: "Ye must be born again." He said that human nature must have a renaissance, a turn-about, it must be changed.

You find lying, cheating, bigotry, greed, hatred and immorality wherever you go. Go to India, go to China . . I defy you to go any place in the world where you don't find these things. It is a disease of human nature, and the Bible calls it sin. Jesus Christ said that a man must be born again, he must have a change of human nature, he must be transformed. And Jesus said that He could do it.

You say, "Well, Billy, that is too simple." I know it sounds simple, and it also sounds illogical, and it may not be very academic.

Nicodemus asked Jesus: "How can these things be?" Jesus answered: Marvel not, Nicodemus, you will never understand it. And then the word that followed is faith. "Faith" is used ninety-two times in one book of the

Bible alone. And by faith, the Bible promises, if we receive Christ into our hearts as Saviour, Lord and Master, we can have our lives changed and transformed.

When I first heard that I; laughed, as some of you are smiling inside now, although I knew that human nature needed a transformation. The necessity of the re-birth was taught by Wesley and Whitefield, and it led Britain into a religious revival that saved Britain from a bloody revolution such as France was having-almost all historians agree to that. It was an old word that John Whitefield and John Wesley used over and over again: "Ye must be born again." What was meant by that? I laughed at it-I said it couldn't happen.

Then one day I said: I am going to give it a trial. So one night, without emotion (it is not an emotional experience, though it can be), very calmly and very quietly I said: All right, God, I am going to give You a trial. I am going to do what You said to do. I am going to tell You I am willing. I don't have the strength, but I am willing to turn from my, sins, and I am really ready to open my heart to You.

When I did that, something happened in my life. I can't explain it to you, I can't analyze it, I can't put it in a test tube. But I will give you one illustration. I come from the part of the country where men look with bias on those who have different coloured skins than they have, and there is discrimination. When I received Christ, I began to look through different eyes at men of different races, and the colour was gone. There was one of God's creatures, no matter what colour skin or shape of nose he had, and the racial prejudice was gone. I began to love instead of to be prejudiced. My life was changed. It didn't become perfect, and it is not perfect today, but I realized I had a new strength, a new power and a new dynamic for living that gave me the ability to say "No" to temptations that normally come. I had found a new resource.

It wasn't the type of religion that gives one a long face and droopy shoulders. It put a smile on my face, it gave me a spring in my step, a joy in my soul, and the happiness and the peace I longed and looked for.

I have seen men of every walk of life try it. I have seen lords and ladies and royalty, I have seen congressmen and senators, I have seen university professors give their lives to Christ. It has happened right here in Toronto in the last few days. One of your professors at the University of Toronto shook my hand last night and said: "Billy, for the last five days I have been living! I didn't know what living was. I would have laughed at this whole thing two weeks ago, but my life is different. I can't explain it. Some of my friends laugh at me, but my life is different."

Why? Because you are a soul, as well as a body and a mind, you will never find an inward joy, peace, forgiveness and sense of security with God until your soul has been satisfied; and your soul cannot be satisfied apart from God.

Now, how would that affect world affairs, you ask. This is an Empire Club . . . we are interested in discussing political and economic affairs. How can that solve the problems of the world?

Let me ask you this: Do you see any solution during the next hundred years to the problems we face the way we are going? How many of you would agree with me when I tell you that as long as men lie and hate and cheat, as long as there is prejudice and greed in the world, there is the possibility that at X point, somewhere out there, some madman will push a button and make the whole world his funeral pyre? Don't you think Hitler would have done it in his last days if he had had the power?

All right. Suppose we could give the whole world an injection of love instead of hate, suppose we could find a serum we could give the human race that would change them over night . . . do you know any serum like that? It is certainly not education alone, because it was the educated in the civilized nations who fought it out in the last war-it wasn't the primitive nations.

Do you know any answer? The answer I am giving today you may not accept-that is your privilege. It is one answer. I believe it is the answer: that human nature can be transformed. Your life can be transformed. If enough people receive Christ and have their lives transformed by His power, I believe it would make an impact on world affairs.

I am not in favour of war, but neither am I in favour of appeasement. I am in favour of a third force that is very rarely mentioned: I am in favour of gathering such a spiritual and moral force in the world that it will make its weight felt in the affairs of men, that we will have such a religious renaissance in the Western World-and in the whole world, for that matter-that we will demand of our leaders "peace in our time". I believe it can be done. I believe there are many evidences that it is happening in Great Britain, it is happening in Germany, it is happening in the United States, and I believe it is happening in Canada, because men today are beginning to turn back to God, back to the church and back to the Bible. I believe it is the only road out of the confusion and bewilderment that we face today.

There is a picture of a chess game hanging in Paris. On one side of the painting is the Devil, and on the other side is a lad about sixteen years of age. They are playing chess. The Devil has a leering, triumphant expression on his face. He has just licked this boy at chess, and the boy is sitting there with his head bowed and big tears trickling down his cheeks. The Devil has just won in the game of life over this lad. He has no strength, he has no way out, and he has given up. The title of the picture is "Check Mate". He had him.

A famous chess player came through one day. He looked at the painting. He felt sorry for the boy and he hated the looks of the Devil. He began to study the board where the men were placed, and all of a sudden he shouted: "Son, I have found a move, one move . . . if you will make that move you can lick the Devil." He forgot himself, he forgot it was a painting-he was so engrossed in it.

We see all the men of chess in the game of life there, and in some of our lives it seems the Devil has almost got us. We look at the whole world picture ... it seems dark at times with its little bright intervals, but by and large the basic issues have not changed, in spite of the recent smiles on both sides of the Iron Curtain. We see the shadow of the hydrogen bomb and all the vast and terrible weapons being created behind scientific laboratories, and, as we look into the future of the next two or three generations, it seems that we are almost ready to say "Check Mate."

But I believe there is One looking down from above who looks upon the board and says to you and me: There is a move, there is one move that you can make, and you can win! That move is toward Jesus Christ. You can make that move today in your own souls.

Chapter 2 - Christ's Answer to the World

Charlotte Crusade. September 21 - 1958

Now, today I will turn to the 17th chapter of the book of Acts, beginning at verse 30. Beginning tomorrow evening I am going to ask how many have brought their Bibles. I want everybody to bring a Bible. Now, I'm not a Bibliographist [sic]. I am not asking you to worship with the Bible. I don't use the Bible as a fetish. But I believe that the Bible is God's inspired Word, and in this book we find God's message for us today. I want you to get in the habit of carrying your Bible, reading your Bible, searching the Scriptures with me.

I am not here night after night to put on a show. We are not here to put on an entertainment. We are here to tell you what the Bible has to say. What does the Bible have to say about your problems? What does the Bible have to say about the problems we're facing in the world in which we live today? Night after night, I'm going to ask you to bring your Bibles.

Now you may have just a little Testament; you might not have a Bible at all. Go downtown and get a Bible. If you don't have the money to get a Bible, Beverly Shea will lend you the money. But get a Bible. Bring your Bibles to the services every evening.
In New York, a lot of people brought great big family Bibles that they could hardly carry. Whatever kind of Bible you have, bring it. We're here to study the Bible and see what the Bible has to say. Everybody has a Bible, but very few people know what the Bible says. We don't know what the Bible says; we don't read its pages. The Bible is an uninteresting closed book. I want us to open the Bible together and see what the message of this book is for the day in which we live. The 17th chapter of the book of Acts:

"But now God commandeth all men every where to repent: because he hath appointed a day, in . . . which he will judge the world in righteousness by that

man whom he hath ordained; whereof he hath given assurance unto all men, in that he hath raised him from the dead. And when they heard of the resurrection of the dead, some mocked: and others said, We will hear thee again of this matter. So Paul departed from among them. Howbeit certain men clave unto him and believed" [verses 30-34].

Here we have a picture of the apostle Paul. He is going throughout the Mediterranean world proclaiming the good news to people in frustration, fear, and sin. And the apostle Paul is preaching Christ to the people, and now he comes to Athens.

Athens was the cultural and intellectual center of the ancient world. It was the city of Plato, Aristotle, and Epicurus. If you take all the universities of America and roll them into one, you have what Athens was to the intellectual world of that day. As in this day, in the midst of intellectual achievements and scientific advances, there existed both confusion and frustration. Greece at that time was under the iron heel of Rome, and the whole world was longing for freedom. They were searching for an answer.

And things haven't changed very much in two thousand years. The world is still searching for an answer. Much of the world is still in slavery. Today Charlotte is considered in the Carolinas one of our intellectual cities. It is considered a city of church-going people. It is considered a religious city. This city is considered an educational center.

The Scriptures say that Paul became spurred on by what he saw. I think the world of our day is also crying for help, as the people in that day were crying for help. The philosophical world is saying, "Come and help us" to the church.

Jean Sartre, who is one of the leaders in modern existentialism, has said, "If you don't believe in God, that's all right. I don't believe in God. But," he said, "believe in something, because man is so philosophically constituted that he needs something to believe in."

So the world of philosophy today for the first time in centuries is crying out to the church, "Help us, give us an answer, we are confused."

The economic world is crying out. Look at India. In India today there are nearly 400 million people – in 1957 (1100 million people – 2007- ed) , increasing at the rate of 5 million a year. Just the problem of population increase alone is bringing about economic pressures that could bring about revolution and trouble in the world to come. Japan has a population of 93 million living on a land area the size of the state of California, increasing at the rate of 1 million a year. China is increasing at the rate of 9 million a year. In twenty-five years, one out of every five babies born in the world will be a Chinese.

The scientific world is crying out, "Help us." Life magazine said not long ago there is a crisis in science. The faster the universe expands, the greater are the areas of ignorance it seems to open. Science has created Frankenstein monsters and doubts its moral ability to control them. We have hydrogen bombs that are ready to be unleashed upon the world.

We are seeing a hardening American attitude. We are seeing verbal blasts back and forth between Russia and America. How long it will only be in the talking phase we do not know, but we do know that our scientists and military leaders are warning that we could be in a nuclear war at any time that could wipe out 60 million Americans in the first few hours.

The political world is crying for help. Communism and democracy, the East and the West, are at each other's throats with two diametrically opposed political ideologies. And the whole political world is saying, "Help us."

A European leader said a few weeks ago, "If the devil could offer a panacea, I would follow the devil." The world is becoming desperate, the world wants an answer, and the world wants an answer quickly.

Thank God that Martin Luther King, who was stabbed last night in New York, was not stabbed by a white person. If he had been, we might have seen a racial war in New York with blood flowing down the street.

Our problems and our tensions are so complicated. No one has the answer. What is the answer? Many people are crying for answers to these problems. The moral problem, mental breakdowns, and other problems arise.

A new word has entered our vocabulary called "escapism." We Americans are trying to escape from reality. We are taking dope, drink, tranquilizing pills, entertainment, and intent upon soul-forgetfulness. People flee from themselves to become lost in the clouds.

And the heroes of modern pictures and films are spiritually homeless. Look at the television programs. How many deal with psychological cases? Every time you look at Gunsmoke [a televsion Western of the time] it sets a psychological problem dressed in western clothes. And I read the other day that the psychiatrists are now going to each other for help.

Edward [Edwin] Arlington Robinson says, "I cannot find my way. There is no star."

Winston Churchill threw up his hands some time ago and said, "Our problems are beyond us."

Paul looked at the confusion of his day in Athens. And the Bible says that Paul was disturbed by what he saw and felt. Ladies and gentlemen, on this warm September afternoon in 1958 I am disturbed by what I see and what I feel. We stand on the brink of catastrophe. Mr. Nehru, speaking to the Indian Parliament, recently said, "We stand on the brink of hell."

Our leaders are warning us, but we have become dead. Our minds are blinded, our wills are paralyzed, and our consciences dulled.

We are so taken up with our money-making, so taken up with the amusements and places and comforts of modern American life, that we don't realize that the forces of evil are closing in round about us. Unless we can turn to God and have His help, we are done for as a nation and as a people.

I do not think that the Charlotte crusade ought to be "another crusade." I do not think it ought to be a crusade kept in the history of the crusades of our team. I think it ought to be something different. I think it ought to be the beginning of a revival throughout the South that can sweep the nation. I think it ought to be something that will set an example to the world and say to the world, "We have an answer. We can solve our problems at the foot of the cross as a community, and we have found an answer to our individual needs in Jesus Christ."

While Paul was disturbed by all this, some of the philosophers came and said, "Paul, we've been listening to you talk. We'd like to hear more of it. How about going up to Mars Hill and giving a lecture?" [See Acts 17:18,19.] And so Paul did. He went up to Mars Hill, and there he preached his famous sermon on Mars Hill. Some people have said that this sermon was a great failure in Paul's life. Some people said that Paul, in preaching this sermon, did not get any results, never founded a great church in Athens, and he never had any persecution and never had any opposition in Athens.

One of the things that disturbs me here is the devil is too quiet. I hope he'll get stirred up somewhere. Because when he is quiet I know he is getting ready to kick us from behind somewhere, while we are not looking.

Every successful work of God must have opposition.

If it doesn't have opposition, there is something wrong with it. Everywhere Paul went he stirred up opposition. Trouble came, and trouble always follows the preaching of the Gospel of Christ, because Satan doesn't like it.

The forces of evil do not like the searchlight pointed in their direction, because "men loved darkness . . . because their deeds [are] evil" [John 3:19].

That day Paul had a great audience out before him in Athens as we have here today. The Athenians had hundreds of different gods and religions. And Charlotte is a very religious city. I'm told that there is one church in this city to every four hundred people, and I do not believe that is equaled anywhere in the world. Not even Edinburgh, Scotland, has as many churches per capita. You are to be congratulated. Thank God.

And, yet, in this city you have one of the highest crime rates in America. What's wrong? Why doesn't it balance out? It may be that we need a revival within our churches. There are thousands of people today who have their name on a church roll that I do not believe have ever made a true commitment to Jesus Christ.

Thousands of people who have been named in the church, who go to church once in awhile--if it's not too inconvenient. And they sit for an hour, and they give God one hour. And they say, "O God, how lucky you are to get me for one hour a week." And the rest of the week they live for the devil and live for themselves, and they claim to be Christians. I tell you, in God's sight those people are not Christians. A Christian is a person in whom Christ dwells, and a Christian is a person who lives Christ twenty-four hours a day.

Paul was preaching to a very religious people. Now the Epicureans were there. The Epicureans were a very strange lot of people, and yet they were not so strange--because there are Epicureans here today. The Epicureans are the people who believe that happiness is the goal of life. Eat, drink, be merry, have a good time. Enjoy yourself, be religious, but don't go too far in religion. Have a good time. They spent more time in front of their television sets than they did reading the Bible, if they had television sets in that day. They spent more time reading the newspapers than they did the Bible. They spent more time in the theater than they did in the church. They go to a double feature at a drive-in theater and sit for four hours and think it's too short. They go to church and listen to a twenty-minute sermon and think it's too long. And to some people, because Sunday is a different day and because you do go to church, you can't wait until Monday when business starts again.

I was just reading the life of Robert Murray McCheyne, that great menace to the church of Scotland a hundred years ago. Robert Murray McCheyne, in preaching on the Sabbath day said, "Scotland will be lost if she loses her belief in keeping the Lord's day totally unto God."

We've lost all concept of God's day.

And I want to tell you people who are counting on getting to heaven: Heaven is going to be one long eternal Sabbath day. And in hell there will be no Sabbath days.

There are a lot of you who, if you got to heaven, heaven would be hell for you, because you don't like the Sabbath. And you don't like to keep the Lord's day in the Lord's way. I believe that we need to get old-fashioned in keeping the Lord's day.

And so the audience was there. The Epicureans said, "Have a good time." Everybody is saying that today. Why, in some of our dairy barns today, they even have the radio going so that the cows can dance a tune while they're giving the milk. Everybody has to be entertained. The radio has to blare, the television has to be on, a magazine has to be in one hand and chewing gum in the mouth with a few aspirins thrown in between. And we say we're having a good time. What a society of people we are. No wonder we are told about deterioration today.

I wish every one of you could have read about two weeks ago the front-page editorial in the morning newspaper in Philadelphia, about the need for return to discipline in our lives and keeping of the Ten Commandments and the Sermon on the Mount.

The Stoics were also there in Paul's audience that day. Now the Stoics were proud and self-righteous. They were the intellectual snobs. They didn't need God. They didn't need a personal experience with Christ. They were self-righteous. And I tell you that we are in danger of being like the Pharisees of old. The most scathing denunciation that Jesus had was against the Pharisees and their self-righteousness. The sins that God hates the most are the sins of pride and self-righteousness. The Bible concludes that we are all sinners.

Paul stood up to that crowd to preach his sermon. And the first thing that Paul said was this: "There is one God." He said, "I saw an inscription coming up this mountain that said, 'To the unknown God.' Oh, I perceive that you are religious people. You believe in some sort of God, but you don't know Him." [See Acts 17:22.]

And there are many of us today that believe in God, but we really don't know Him. When we wake up in the morning, His presence does not instill our room. When we go to bed at night, our last thought is not on Him. When we go to pray, we spend so little time, and we get no answers to our prayers. And God means so little to us. We go to church because it's the traditional thing and social thing. We don't go because we really love Christ. We've never had a true experience with Him until He fills our lives.

Paul said, "I want to tell you about this God" [verse 23]. Yet, we are becoming conscious of God today. The Bible tells us that God is creator and preserver of the universe [see Genesis 1:1]. But the Bible says, "God is a Spirit" [John 4:24]. The Bible says God is unchanging. The Bible says that God does not change one iota. He doesn't change the batting of an eyelash.

[See Malachi 3:6.] God is the same yesterday, today, and forever [see Hebrews 13:8].

We have an idea in this country that God is changed to accommodate Himself for Americans.

We have an idea that we Americans are God's chosen people, that God loves us more than any other people,
and that we are God's blessed. I tell you that God doesn't love us any more than He does the Russians. He doesn't love us any more than He does the Chinese. He doesn't love us any more than He does the Africans. God doesn't love us any more than any other people. There is no changing with God, and there is no partiality with God.

The Bible says God is righteous [see Psalm 145:17]. And there are a lot of you who can't understand the Old Testament when you read it. You know why? Because the Old Testament is teaching one thing: The Old Testament is teaching the holiness and the righteousness of God. You'll never understand it until you understand that God was teaching that He is a holy God. And no sin can come into God's presence because He's holy [see Habakkuk 1:13]. God is a holy and righteous God. And the Bible says that God will judge the world [see Acts 17:31].

We have an idea today that God is like a Santa Claus, sitting on a cloud somewhere with a harp in His hand, forgiving everybody. God is not like that at all. God is a God of judgment. He is the God of righteousness and holiness, and the Bible says here that He will not wink at sin [see Acts 17:30,31]. You think that you can get away with your lying. I'll tell you, you cannot. You think you can get away with your cheating. I tell you, you cannot. You think you can get away with your adultery, your jealousy, your sins, and the lust in your heart, and the evil thoughts that you have, and the evil moments that you have. I tell you, God says we shall be judged.

The Bible says, "All have sinned, and come short of the glory of God" [Romans 3:23].

I am a sinner and you are a sinner. Every one of us is a sinner in God's sight.

But the Bible also tells us that God is a God of love.

"For God so loved the world, that he gave his only begotten Son, that whosoever believeth in him, should not perish, but have everlasting life" [John 3:16].

The Bible tells us God commended His love to us and that "while we were yet sinners, Christ died for us" [Romans 5:8].

The Bible tells us that because God is love, He created man. Why did God create us in the first place? He put us here and He created us because He is love and He wanted to have an object to love; and so He created the human race. We were perfect, and we had fellowship with God. Adam and Eve walked with God in the cool of the day. They were friends. God and man were friends. They walked together, they talked together, they planned together. But then one day something happened, because when God created you, He gave you the ability to choose between right and wrong. He gave you the ability to choose whether you would follow God and serve God, or whether you would live your own life and build your own life apart from God. When man came to that great decisive moment in his life, he turned away from God and decided that he could build his own life without God. And he broke his covenant with God; he broke his relationship with God; he sinned against God. [See Genesis 2,3.]

And that's the reason we have war today. That's the reason we have racial tension today. That's the reason we have all these problems in the world today. It is because the hearts of men are sinful. We are away from God. And that's the reason you have the problems in your personal life that you can't solve. That's the reason there are things within your own heart that you don't understand.

God, looking down from heaven one day, saw this earth in its turmoil and strife and sinfulness, saw us in our lost condition, saw us in our sins. And the Bible says that God said, "I love you. I love you. I love you. I want to save you."

But how could God? He fills all of space. He is the mighty God of creation that flung those billions of stars out into space. So God did something that astounded the universe. God became a man. That's who Jesus Christ was. He was God. And when I see Jesus making the blind to see, I see God. When I see Jesus feeding the five thousand, I see God interested in the hunger and the desires of men. When I see Jesus dying on the cross,

I see God in Christ reconciling the world unto Himself. I see the nails in His hands. I see the spike in His feet. I see the crown of thorns on His brow. I hear Him say, "My God, my God, why hast thou forsaken me?" [see Matthew 27:46]. In that terrible moment, Jesus was separated from God in a mysterious way that none of us understood. And now God said, "This is my Son, in whom I am well pleased. Believe in Him. Receive Him. And I will save you." [See Matthew 17:5.]

But Jesus didn't stay on the cross. They put Him in the tomb, and on the third day He rose again. And I do not offer you this afternoon a dead Christ. I offer you a risen Christ, a Christ that is at the right hand of God the Father, and who is some day going to come to judge the quick and the dead [see Acts 10:41,42]. I offer you a triumphant Christ who is going to win.

A lot of people say, "Do you think communism is going to win the world?" They might win it temporarily, but it will only be temporarily. Because the Bible says that Jesus Christ is going to establish His kingdom, and the church shall some day triumph. Some day those of us who know Christ shall reign with Him [see Revelation 5:10]. God within Christ is reconciling the world unto Himself [see

2 Corinthians 5:19]. But God said, "I gave my Son to die."

Now there are three things you have to do to get to heaven and have your sins forgiven; if you're to have Christ in your life, and if you're to have a new life and a transformed nature, if you're to have your sins forgiven. If you're to go to heaven, you're going to have to do three things. I've studied this Bible for twenty years, and I do not believe any man or woman will get to heaven who hasn't done these three things. I don't care who you are. You may be a Sunday school teacher, you may be a deacon, an elder, or a steward. I don't care who you are. If you haven't done these three things, I do not believe you can get to heaven.

First, you must repent of your sins.

The Scripture says in this passage, "God. . .commandeth all men every where to repent" [Acts 17:30]. That's not a command from me. I didn't say it. I want to ask you tonight, or this afternoon, have you repented? Has there been a time in your life when you repented? You might have been confirmed, you might have been baptized; and you might be born again in your heart, but you're not sure of it. You're not certain of it. You're not sure that there has ever been a moment when you really repented of your sins and renounced them. You can do it today.

"What do you mean by repentance?" I mean that you ac-

knowledge to God that you have sinned, and that you are willing to turn from your sins. Notice I said willing. You may not have the strength to turn from your sins, but by faith you are willing to turn if God will give you the strength. You say, "Billy, there are things in my life that are wrong, but I cannot give them up. I've tried. I just can't do it." If you are willing, God will give you the strength to give them up and turn from them.

Secondly, you must receive Christ by faith;

An act of receiving Christ to die for you. Now that is a definite act. It may be unconscious, or it may be conscious. It may be a quiet moment; it may be a decisive, climactic moment as it was in the life of Paul.

But if you're not sure by faith you've received Christ, you'd better do it today.

There are three little men who live inside us all-- our intellect, our emotions, and our will. Intellectually, thousands of you believe in Christ. I doubt if there is anyone here who doesn't believe in Christ. You believe in Him with your minds. In fact, the Bible says the devil believes. And the devil does more than you do, because he trembles when he believes the Bible [see James 2:19]. But that's not enough. You may have some emotion in your religion. You may have had an emotional experience at some time, but you never have really received Christ. You must by faith receive Him, because it is an act of your will. You say, "I will trust Him, I will follow."

You know why I ask people to come forward in our meeting to receive Christ? Because all the way through the Scriptures, I learned that God wanted people to do something as a testimonial of their faith. When Jesus healed the man with the withered arm, He could have said, "Be healed," and he would have been healed. But He didn't do it. He said, "Stretch it forth," and the man stretched it forth. Now he had tried to stretch it forth many times, but he couldn't. But at the behest of Jesus, he did stretch it forth and it was healed. [See Matthew 12:10-13.] Jesus wanted him to do something. I am asking you to come today to give your life to Christ, to do something, to receive Christ who trusts you.

The third thing you must do: You must obey Christ.

You must be willing to follow Him and serve Him from this moment on. Follow and serve Him. It means self-denial, it means cross-bearing, it means obedience. It means that you are going to burn all of your bridges behind you and follow Christ, no matter what it costs. It means you go back to your business and back to your home and live Christ, no matter what it costs. It means you are going to renew your vows to the church. It means you are going to be faithful and loyal to your church as never before. You are going to start tithing to the church.

It means you are going to start praying in your home. It means you are going to start living for Christ, no matter what the costs, from this moment on. That's what it means. And if you are not willing to do that, don't come to Jesus Christ. He will not accept you just part of the way. You must be willing to go all the way.

When Paul had finished his sermon he stopped. And when the invitation was given that day, three things took place that are going to take place here this afternoon. One, there was derision. Some of them laughed at him and mocked him [see Acts 17:32]. They didn't mock him out loud; just quietly and sighed, "Well, that's not for me."

Somebody said I had come to Charlotte to try to get everybody in the Baptist church. I heard about a fellow with a cat some time ago. He was trying to sell a little kitten. He was taking it up and down the street.

And he said, "This is a Baptist kitten, a Baptist kitten for sale." And he couldn't sell it. The next day he came around, he said, "It's a Methodist kitten." The man said, "Why, these are the same kittens as yesterday. Why do you call them Methodist kittens?" "Well, today they've got their eyes open."

You may be a Baptist, a Presbyterian, or Methodist, or Episcopal, or Moravian, or a Lutheran, or a Catholic, or Jew. But if you have never really had a vital encounter with Jesus Christ, you make sure today.

Secondly, there were some who said, "We will hear again of this matter" [see verse 32]. They put it off. Governor Felix said to Paul, "Go thy way for this time; when I have a convenient season, I will call for thee" [Acts 24:25]. I want to tell you, this is a dangerous action because you may never hear anyone present the Gospel again. Some of the philosophers were never able to climb Mars Hill again.

The Bible says,

"He that hardeneth his heart, being often reproved, shall suddenly be cut off and not without remedy" [see Proverbs 29:1].

You never know. To some of you who go out on the slick highways this afternoon, this may be the last sermon you will ever hear. In every crusade we have ever conducted anywhere, there have been people who have come to the meeting in good health and never came back because they were dead in the next few hours through an accident, or a heart attack, or something else.

We never know when our moment is coming. Maybe God spoke to you this afternoon, and your heart is in danger of being hardened. Some of you are older people; some of you are younger people. The Bible says once you hear the Gospel and do nothing about it, you are in danger of being hardening your heart.

But, last of all, there were some that made a decision [see Acts 17:34]. They received Christ and went their way rejoicing. I am going to ask you today to receive Him. I am not asking you this afternoon to join some special church. I'm asking you today to give your life to Christ.

You may be a member of a choir. I don't know who you are or what you are, but you want to give your life to Christ on this opening Sunday afternoon. I'm going to ask you to do a hard thing, because coming to Christ is not easy. So many people have made it too easy. Jesus went to the cross and died in your place. Certainly, you can come a few steps from where you are sitting and stand here, quietly and reverently, and with bowed head. And say, "I need God; I need Christ. I want to be forgiven of my sins. I want a new life, and I want to start a new direction today."

You may be a rich man;
you may be a poor man.

You may be a man of great intellectual capacities, and you have to come by faith.

Because you'll never understand it all intellectually.

If you want to...... come to the cross and give your life to Christ,

I'm going to ask you to come. If you are with friends and relatives, they'll wait on you. There's plenty of time and I'm going to ask not a person to leave the Coliseum.

Chapter 3 - The World's Darkest Hour

October 18, 1958 Charlotte, North Carolina

Now Matthew, the 26th chapter, beginning at the 36th verse: "Then cometh Jesus with them unto a place called Gethsemane, and saith unto the disciples, Sit ye here, while I go and pray yonder. And he took with him Peter and the two sons of Zebedee, and began to be sorrowful and very heavy. Then saith he unto them, My soul is exceeding sorrowful, even unto death: tarry ye here, and watch with me. And he went a little farther, and fell on his face, and prayed, saying, O my Father, if it be possible, let this cup pass from me: nevertheless, not as I will, but as thou wilt" [verses 36-39].

I want you to see this picture tonight .

Because the last twenty-four hours in the life of Christ was the darkest period in the history of the entire world.

Here we find an incident in the last hours of the life of Christ which I want us to think about tonight and see what practical application we have in our own lives and the world in which we live.

Many people write to me and say, "We do not understand the Gospel. We do not understand what you mean by receiving Christ or being born again." But I think more people write to me and say this:

They do not understand why Christ had to die on the cross in order for us to be saved. They do not understand the dark hours of Gethsemane. They do not understand why Christ voluntarily laid down His life. They do not understand why He endured the shame of the cross. They do not understand all the phrases in the Bible that talk about the blood.

Many times in the Scriptures you find the phrase,

"the blood of Christ" [Hebrews 9:14];
"the blood of Christ cleanses us from all sin"
 [see 1 John 1:7].

People revolt against that. They do not like that, and they wonder why that is in the Bible. They wonder why so much stress is placed upon the crucifixion and the resurrection of Jesus Christ. Tonight I want us to see that these last twenty-four hours in the life of Christ were the darkest in history, yet it was the darkness just before the dawn.

I believe that history repeats itself.

And when the world comes to that moment of despair--that moment when it is about to blow itself apart, that moment when it seems there is no solution-- at that moment, the sun will rise. The kingdom of God shall come because we have the promise in the Scripture that Jesus Christ, the Son of the living God, is coming back to this earth again. He is going to set up His kingdom and then shall the prayer be answered as He taught in the Lord's Prayer, "Thy kingdom come" [Matthew 6:10]. His kingdom shall rule.

But before the triumph, before the crown, before the kingdom, before the victory, there had to come the suffering. Before you can share in Christ's victory, before you can have a new life here and now, before you can go to heaven, before you can claim the promise that we shall someday reign with Christ, you, too, must come to that same cross. You, too, must come in simple faith and stand at the foot of that cross and receive the Saviour who was willing to go to the cross.

I want you to see Him on this night before He died.

He has had the last supper with the disciples in the upper room, and they have gone now to the Mount of Olives. Now they are in the garden that is called Gethsemane. And Jesus leaves eight of His disciples on the outskirts of the garden and He takes three with Him--Peter, James and John. He goes a little further into the garden, and He tells these three disciples to watch and pray. Then He goes about a stone's throw farther along and falls prostrate on the ground and begins the agonizing prayer. Before He was finished, the Bible says He sweat, as it were, great drops of blood [see Luke 22:44].

What agony! How Christ must have prayed that night. Many times in Scripture you find Christ praying all night. If Jesus Christ had to pray all night, what about us in 1958? With our race problems, with our problem of communism, with the problem of crime that is getting worse with every passing day, with all the social problems that we face in the world and the personal problems and the problem of sin, we Americans are not praying. We are not calling upon God. We give lip service to God, but our hearts are far from Him [see Matthew 15:8].

Why, when the President of the United States gave a proclamation for a day of prayer the other day, you did not read very much about it. Very few churches observed it. Very few people spent any time in prayer. When the President said we should call on God, the people did not call on God.

We cannot call ourselves a Christian nation tonight.

There are Christians living in America, and Christian influences have been felt in this country; but we today are a heathen, pagan country. We are away from God. We have beautiful churches, but our hearts are far from God. We are not spending time in prayer. The blackest hour in history since the last twenty-four hours of the life of Christ we are living in today. We are living on the brink of hell itself, living on the brink of annihilation. And we are not praying. We are not calling upon God.

Jesus prayed and agonized until blood drops came out from Him. That night Jesus prayed a mysterious prayer, an unusual prayer, a strange prayer. He said, "O God, if it be possible, let this cup pass from me. Nevertheless, not my will, but thine, be done." What did He mean by that prayer, "Let this cup pass from me"?

A cup of medicine is offered to a child, and he shrinks back. Then, at the bidding of his father, he takes it. That night a bitter cup was offered to Jesus, and He shrank from it. Why? I want you to see it tonight. Always the cross had been before Christ since the day He was at His baptism [see John 1:29]; at the temptation [see Matthew 4:1-11]; and at the marriage of Cana when He said, "My hour is not yet come" [see John 2:1-4]; when the crowd wanted to make Him a king at the Mount of Transfiguration, when He talked to Elijah and Moses [see Matthew 17:1-4]. He knew that He must die.

He told His disciples He must go to the cross. He read in the Old Testament Scriptures about the suffering the Messiah must endure. The shadow of the cross was before Him all the time. He knew that He had to go to the cross to pay for our sins if we were to be saved. But here was the final hour, and the cup of suffering was bitter.

In order for us to understand the chemical formula of the elixir of the cup that night, I want us to look into it deeply for a moment. I want us to see it and analyse it. I want us to see how much Christ endured that we might be forgiven of sin, that we might go to heaven, that we might have some hope of the solution of our problems.

The first element in that cup was physical pain.

Men had died terrible deaths before. Men had been thrown into boiling water; men had been burned at the stake. Other men had died and suffered physical pain. But the death of the cross was something even worse than that. The death of the cross is said to be the worst possible torture that a man can endure. Because, first, they would strip a man to the waist. Then they would tie his hands together and bend him over and take long leather thongs with lead pellets or steel pellets embedded in the leather thongs, and beat him across the back until his back was in ribbons. And many times the lash of those thongs would come around his face and take his eyes out by the sockets, even tear his teeth out. Often death followed just the scourging and the floggings that were given by great muscular men. Jesus endured that kind of flogging for you and for me.

Then they took a crown of thorns and placed it on His brow, and His face bled as they jerked His beard off. Then they spat in His face until He was covered from head to foot with the spittle of the people. Hatred, prejudice, intolerance, bigotry, all that the human heart could devise against Christ. Christ was not killed by Rome or Israel.

The Bible tells us that Christ was crucified by you and me; my sins and your sins crucified Christ. We had a part in it, all the hatred of mankind.

We have seen in the past few days what hatred can do. We have seen how some men with sticks of dynamite can blow up synagogues just to express their hate. May God have mercy upon them. The human heart is expressed in that cross as they flogged Him, as they beat Him, as they spit on Him, as they put a crown of thorns on Him.

Then they gave Him a 250-pound cross to carry. He stumbled along the road with that cross until Simon of Cyrene had to come and help Him carry the cross [see Mark 15:21]. And I am certain Simon, today in heaven, is thrilled and proud of the fact that he helped Jesus carry the cross. Have you helped Jesus to carry the cross, or were you one of those putting nails in His hands?

You say, "But, Billy, I would never put a nail in Jesus' hands. I would never flog Him." Wouldn't you? You did it today! The sin that you committed today helped to crucify Christ because those people were all representative. We were expressing ourselves in them. You and I helped crucify Jesus. He was dying for our sins.

Then they took Him to Golgotha's mountain, and they put spikes in His hands. They tore His hands. They tore His hands and His feet. He never uttered a sound. The pain, the thirst--His tongue was swollen double. He hung hour upon hour on that terrible cross. Then at the end--many times when a person is dying on a cross the ravenous birds, the vultures, would come with their iron-like beaks and pick at him while he was still alive. That was the cross.

And night--the night before He died, Jesus was on His knees before God and saying, "O God, if it is possible to save Billy Graham, if it is possible to save Jim Jones, if it is possible to save men and women some other way without me having to endure that pain, O God, find it."

But there was another suffering. There was the suffering of loneliness,

Because Jesus went to the cross alone. No one else could go with Him. He was the Son of God. He was the only one in the universe who could bear all of our sins. He was the Paschal Lamb that Passover season, and the lamb had to be without blemish [see Exodus 12:5]. He was the Paschal Lamb being slain from the foundation of the world for our sins [see Revelation 13:8]. He alone had in His body and His soul the capacity to bear our sins.

Because, you see, we had sinned against God. We had rebelled against God, and we deserve death and we deserve judgment and we deserve hell. But Jesus said, "I will take the judgment, I will take the hell, and I will take the suffering." And He went to that cross alone because only He could suffer. Only He could be offered as a sacrifice that would be pleasing to God and would reconcile God and man together. So He endured it alone.

Judas was betraying Him for thirty pieces of silver, about twenty-one dollars [see Matthew 26:14-16]. You have betrayed Him today. The lie you told betrayed Jesus, the lustful thoughts that you have, the immoral deed that you did, the cheating that you did in business. How many times we have betrayed Him! We were a part of that betrayal and are just as guilty as Judas. And we will go to the same place as Judas went unless we repent of our sins and come to Jesus Christ and ask Him to forgive us.

Jesus died alone. The disciples forsook Him, and Peter denied Him. There He is, alone and hanging on the cross for our sins.

There are many types of loneliness. There is the loneliness of solitude. You have been alone when all you could hear was the thunder of the surf alongside the ocean on some faraway beach. I stood on a lonely beach in India, and I did not see a person for miles. The most beautiful beaches in the world, I think, are along the coral strands of India. I heard only the beating against the surf, against the rocks. Loneliness.

Admiral Byrd wrote in his book how he spent five months in the loneliness and darkness of the South Pole. Louis Zamperini, a friend of ours in California, spent thirty-five days alone on a life raft in loneliness, not knowing at any moment when he might be pulled down by a shark or when a Japanese plane would come and machine-gun him. Loneliness.

There are other types of loneliness. There is the loneliness of society. There is the poor creature who is living in a tenement house in New York tonight watching this telecast. You never receive a letter. You never hear a word of encouragement. You never know the handclasp of a friend. Or there is the wealthy society leader whose money has bought everything but happiness and joy. Or there is the country girl in New York or Los Angeles tonight who is seeking fame and fortune in the big city and has been disillusioned and disappointed, and now she is lonely. There is loneliness in a crowd, and some of you living in the midst of the big city are very lonely tonight. There is an emptiness in your heart.

I want to tell you something. You give your life to Christ tonight and He can become your friend, even closer than a brother [see Proverbs 18:24]. He can be with you in your loneliness.

Then there is the loneliness of suffering.

Some of you are watching from hospital beds right now, from hospitals all over the country; and you are lonely lying there. A lady gave her life to Christ some time ago. And she said, "I've been crippled for five years with arthritis, and I have suffered. What a terrible suffering I have had." Then she added, "I have spent many a day alone, but never a lonely day."

Give your life to Christ, and you need never have a lonely day. Because, you see, Jesus has also suffered. He knows what it means to suffer, and in suffering He understands your suffering. He can come and put His hand on your brow and comfort you, and be there by your side during those lonely hours of suffering.

Then there is the loneliness of sorrow.

You have been in the sickroom and you have seen a loved one snatched from you. You could not do anything about it. Your heart has been crushed by sorrow.

There is disappointment in your life. Maybe your husband has walked out on you. Maybe your boyfriend has left you, and your heart is crushed.

Jesus also suffered, and He knows. He stood at the grave of His friend Lazarus and wept [see John 11-35]. He knows what it means to have a crushing sorrow. He can be there with you right now. He can wipe those tears away. He can give you a joy and peace in your heart and take away that loneliness.

Then there is the loneliness of character.

A man may find himself in a community or a society where he has to take a stand alone on some moral issue. It is not easy to stand alone. Moses had to stand alone [see Exodus 3:13-22]. Elijah on Mount Carmel had to stand alone. Everybody in the country was against Elijah. He was the only man that stood for God. [See 1 Kings 18:17-46.]

The fact is, we who know the Lord Jesus Christ as our Saviour are in a small minority in the world. We are going to be standing more and more alone. Someday we may have to pay with our blood and our life for our faith in Jesus Christ. You are standing alone in your office. You are the only one who is trying to live for Christ on the high school campus. You are the only one in your class. You are the only one in your community trying to live for God. Sometimes you get discouraged and you feel lonely. Well, remember that almost everybody whom God ever used knew those hours of loneliness.

Then there is the loneliness of sin.

That is the worst of all. The Bible says when Judas betrayed Jesus on that last night at the supper, he left the meeting of the disciples and he went out-- because it was night [John 13:30]. You remember when you were young and your conscience was sensitive. If you told a lie, your conscience spoke to you. But now it has become hardened and seared. There are many of you sitting at a bar right now. You wish your life were different. You wish that you were not chained by the habits of sin tonight. You would like to be through but you cannot, although you have tried. Yes, there is loneliness of sin. The older you get the more lonely you will be, because you will be farther away from God. There is nothing but loneliness and remorse.

Go ahead and continue for awhile. The Bible says there is pleasure in sin for a season [see Hebrews 11:25]. You can get away with it for a while.

A man told me one day, "I'm not afraid of going to hell; there are going to be a lot of other people down there." But, listen, the Bible indicates that hell is a lonely place. You won't see anybody else there. You won't even see the devil. A lot of people have an idea that hell is a place where the devil is standing at a furnace and giving the orders, or sitting in a big office running hell. That is not the picture at all.

The picture is one of separation from God and the blackness of night, darkness and loneliness. You will be all alone. You won't see your husband or your wife. You won't see your friends. You will be alone--the loneliness of sin. Sin pays wages [see Romans 6:23]. And it crushes your personality, it crushes your life, it crushes your soul, and it ends up in hell.

Turn to Christ tonight from your sins.

Let Him free you. Let Christ come in, and then heaven will be a place of fellowship with your loved ones. Heaven will be a glorious world of fellowship and friendship. There will be no loneliness in heaven. The Bible says there will be no night there [see Revelation 22:5]. What a hope we have, those of us who know Jesus Christ as our Saviour.

The Bible says Christ suffered alone. "I have trodden the winepress alone; and of the people there was none with me" [Isaiah 63:3], said Jesus.

The third element in this bitter cup was the mental anguish.

Jesus had quoted Isaiah the prophet. Jesus knew He had to suffer. He knew something about the affliction of the next day and that night in the garden. He knew what was going to take place, and naturally He was suffering much anguish as He thought about the suffering of the next day.

We have thousands of people in America who are suffering mentally. We have thousands of psychological problems. We have thousands of people in our mental institutions. We have thousands of people today who are confused mentally. I want to tell you that Jesus can touch your mind if you will let Him come in. Because thousands of our mental problems are the result of spiritual separation from God, or they are the result of idolatry. They are the result of putting other things before God, and that cause's mental unbalance many times. There are thousands of people who are suffering mentally.

Down here in the South there are thousands of people who are suffering anguish at this particular time. It is not just a southern problem. It is a world problem. It is the problem on Cyprus, it is the problem in the Middle

East, it is the problem in New York, it is the problem in Chicago, it is the problem in the Far East, it is the problem in India. Thousands of people are searching their souls. Their minds are tortured and bewildered, wondering what is the right thing to do in such a complicated situation.

I tell you Christ is the answer.
Come to Christ.
Come to the foot of the cross
and let Him touch your mind,
and your heart, and relax your soul.

Then shall we have love for our fellowman, as love knows no bounds, and we shall love our neighbours as ourselves [see Matthew 19:19].

There are thousands of people who want to obey the law, but they don't know what the law is. The federal government says one thing and the state government says another, and they are confused. The tremendous confusion comes because it is a constitutional problem as well as a race problem. Many people are making emotional statements at the moment, flag-waving statements, hysterical statements. Would to God that all of us could come to the cross and see in Christ a solution to all the problems that bewilder us and confuse us.

That may not be your problem. There may be some other problem in your life, but you need Jesus. You need Christ. The country needs Christ.

The fourth element in this bitter cup that Jesus was about to drink was the cup of the anguish of soul.

The physical pain, the loneliness of its shame, and the mental anguish was nothing compared to the spiritual suffering which Jesus Christ suffered on the cross that day. That night He was thinking about God, and His suffering was wrapped up in one little word "sin." Because that next day Jesus was going to become guilty of your sins and my sins. A cloud was going to pass between Him and God--a cloud, for the first time--and

His pure righteous soul was going to be filled with sin. Your sins were going to be laid on Him. The Scripture says that God "had laid on him the iniquity of us all" [Isaiah 53:6]. The Bible says He was "made . . . to be sin for us, who knew no sin" [2 Corinthians 5:21]. He had never known sin, but He was made to be sin.

His soul must have shuddered. His soul must have been shaken. How Jesus must have looked with horror. He said, "O God, if it is possible, let this cup pass from me. O God, I don't want to have to drink this cup. If there is any other way to save men, if there is any other way for the world to be saved, let it be done."

But the Bible says you cannot work for it. The Bible says, "By grace are ye saved through faith; and that not of yourselves: it is the gift of God: not of works, lest any man should boast" [Ephesians 2:8,9]. You can work your fingers to the bone doing good work, but that will not save your soul. You are not saved by works. Suppose a man could pay for it. Suppose you had a billion dollars tonight, suppose you were the richest man in the world, and you gave it all to charity, and you gave it all to God. Would you go to heaven? Not unless you had come to the cross. Because, you see, if you could have bought your way, or if you could have worked your way, or if you could have schemed your way to heaven, Jesus need never have gone to the cross. That night God would have said, "Jesus, you do not have to go to the cross." But God did not say that to His Son. There was no other way.

If I could tell you another way of salvation that is easier, I would tell you. I tell you tonight after studying this book for twenty years, there is no other name given among men whereby we must be saved except the name of Jesus [see Acts 4:12]. There is no other way of salvation except at the foot of the cross.

When I look at the cross tonight,

I see four things.
I see, first, the terribleness of sins. I know that I am a sinner. When I look at Christ dying in my place on the

cross and realize the things that I have done and that it was my sins that nailed Him there, I must cry out to God, "O God, I am a sinner."

The second thing I see is the amazing love of God, that "God commended his love toward us, in that, while we were yet sinners, Christ died for us" [Romans 5:8]. You have rebelled against God, you have sinned against God, you have done things that you know you should not have done. You have helped even crucify Jesus. But in spite of it, God loves you.

And on the cross there is written in gigantic letters in neon fire, "God so loved the world, that he gave his only begotten Son, that whosoever believeth in him should not perish, but have everlasting life" [John 3:16]. There is the love of God. And if you have any doubt concerning the love of God, look at the cross. It was there that He died for us.

The Third, in that cross I find my complete redemption. Christ bowed His head and said, "It is finished" [John 19:30]. I cannot add anything to it. I cannot take anything away. If I am ever to get to heaven, I will have to come to the cross. If I am ever to have my sins forgiven, I will have to come to the cross.

I want to ask you tonight, have you ever been to the cross? Are you sure that you have had this encounter with God at the cross? You may be a member of the church. You may live a moral life. You may be a decent person. I don't know who you are or what you are. It doesn't make any difference where you come from or what your nationality background is, what state you live in, how rich or how poor, how educated or uneducated, you have to come to the cross. Jesus said it's a narrow gate, and the gate is the cross.

If you are not sure that you have been there, renouncing your sin and receiving Christ, you come tonight. Because I do not see how any person can resist the love of God. Many people ask me what is the unpardonable sin. I tell you it is the sin that God cannot pardon. Any man or woman that rejects or resists His

Son, Jesus Christ--that's the unpardonable sin. "There remained no more sacrifice for sins" [Hebrews 10:26]. There is no other way. I tell you, my beloved friends of this great nation, there is only one way of forgiveness and redemption and salvation, and that is the cross of Christ.

I am asking you to come to the cross tonight. I am asking you to come by faith and say, "O God, I have sinned. O God, I am sorry for the things I have done. I am coming by faith to receive thy Son, Jesus Christ." Don't neglect it. Don't put it off until another night. You may never have another moment quite like this tonight.

God says, "I want to meet you. I want to help you. But I'll only meet you and help you at one place, and that is at the cross." It may look foolish for me to say, "Get up out of your seat and come." Don't ask me how it happens. I only know that when a man comes to Christ, he can never be the same again. I only know that his life is changed if he comes to the cross. And I am going to ask you to come right now.

Chapter 4 - Choices

San Jose, California 1981

Tonight I want you to turn with me to the Old Testament to Joshua the 24th chapter. Joshua as you know was a great military leader and he took the place of Moses when Moses went to be with the Lord. And the 15th verse. Now he had called all the leaders of Israel together at a place called Shechem and he's getting ready to die, and this is his farewell address. And during this address he warns the people about their idolatry. He warns them that the judgments of God will fall upon them unless they live for the Lord. And here's what he says:

And *if it seem evil* unto you to serve the LORD, choose you this day whom ye will serve;

... if you want to serve the devil –then serve him, but make a choice. **Whether the gods which your fathers served that were on the other side of the flood,**

or the gods of the Amorites, in whose land ye dwell: but as for me and my house, we will serve the LORD.

Joshua said if every one of you serves other idols, another gods, makes no difference, as for me and my house we've already made a decision: we are going to serve the Lord. And that's a decision that every single person here tonight has to make. You either have to decide that you are going to serve the gods of materialism all around us or the true and the living God.

I'm told that this county has the highest per capita income of any county in the United States. That probably almost means the world. The affluent county that you live in and the area that you live in presents many temptations, because of fluency Jesus warned against the deceitfulness of riches. And he indicated that riches could become a stumbling block to the Kingdom of God. And we have a tremendous responsibility to share our wealth with those that are less fortunate in other parts of the world.

And Joshua was warning the people to choose God, to follow Him instead of these other gods. Julius Caesar ordered by Pompey to disband his legions in goal - had to make a decision: will he take his legions to Rome and become Caesar or will he stay on the other side of the river. He plunged his horse into the river. The die was cast. And he moved on into history. And so we have to make a choice. Moses had warned Israel much earlier, generation earlier, when he was dying he said,

'I call heaven and earth to record this day against you, that I have set before you life and death, blessing and cursing: therefore choose life, that both thou and thy seed may live.'

Moses had said the same things that Joshua is saying separated by many years and every generation has to hear it over and over, and over again. And that's why the Gospel never grows old. It applies to every generation alike. We have to make a choice. Alexander the Great was asked how he conquered the world. He said, **'By not wavering!'** And James says in the first chapter: **For he that wavereth is like a wave of the sea driven with the wind and tossed. He's a double minded man is unstable in all his ways.**

Are you unstable about you relationship to Christ? Do you waver in your relationship to Christ? Are you totally committed to Christ as savior law? Or do you waver about it? Many of you waver by the way you live and Jesus warned the hypocrites: people who pretend one thing and live another. This was his great battle with the hypocrites in the church. We have oldproverbs that are familiar to us all. *He who hesitates* is *lost. Procrastination is the thief of* time. *A stitch in time saves nine. A* bird in the hand is worth two in the bush.

Don't waver! Make a decision! Do it now! That's what Joshua was saying. And Joshua the great military hero that had led them from victory to victory reminded them of all the victories that God had given. And he said, **'Serve God and live! Serve these other gods and you'll die and come under the judgment of God.'**

And the message has not changed. Now the wars were over but Joshua found that the people were going toward idolatry and many times the problems of peace are greater than the problems of war. And he had called all these leaders to Shechem. Now Shechem was the most historical place in all of Israel at that time and still is today. It was where Abraham had first settled when he left earlier. It was where Jacob had purchased his parcel of land. It was where the bones of Joseph had been buried when they were brought up from Egypt. And so he has two mountains there; I've stood there.

And on one mountain he put six of the tribes and on the other mountain he put the other six, and Joshua spoke with a mighty voice even though he was an old man. And he reviews the history of Israel and how God had blessed them. And how they had won their victories not by their own power and their own strategies, and their own ingenuity, and their own strength, but by the power of God. And the people should have been grateful to God, but instead they were now going to other gods.

And we in America should be grateful to God for the blessing he's given us. But what do we find? We find that we are worshipping other gods – the gods of pleasure, the gods of lust and greed, and hate, the gods of materialism, even the gods of war. And Joshua tells them that such a condition cannot continue. They must decide whether they want to serve the idols or to serve the living God. And he will not allow any neutrality; neither does Jesus Christ.

And Joshua said, **'You have to decide immediately. Now.'**Choose you this day, not tomorrow. This day whom you are going to serve. And many of you are going to have to decide tonight what is the #1 priority in your life. Is the priority Christ? Or is the priority something else? Christ demands first place. There is no room on the throne of your heart for two gods. It's either Christ or it's the other god.

There is a man here tonight who is translating for us just tonight in Japanese as we translate every night in the Japanese and Spanish, and many other languages.

And his name is pastor Oda. And he came over from Japan to attend the conference here and he translated for Cliff last year when Cliff would get up to make the announcements about all of our crusades across Japan. And he was reminding me of that great crusade that we held in a stadium like this in Fukuoka and there was a typhoon, and the rain was coming, and the wind was blowing, and the rain was coming in sheets, and it was a beautiful baseball stadium. It seated I think more or as many as this stadium.

There are only a thousand people that profess Christianity in that whole great city of Fukuoka – a city of over a million people. And yet 18 and 19 thousand people came night after night in that typhoon, and sat in that pouring rain, and that wind, and that cold, and heard the Gospel and when the invitations were given they would came in the hundreds. And I made it a point to say that when you come to Christ, you have to give up all other gods. And you know, pastor Oda was telling us a few minutes ago about churches that have doubled and have tripled in size as a result of the crusades.

Because I believe the emphasis must... we must lay it out straight that you cannot serve God and mammon. You must make a choice. And I found that the harder the challenge is the greater the response. Young people today want a challenge. They want something tough and hard, all right? Give your life to Christ. He'll challenge you. Because he says you must deny self and take up a cross. He says, **'I'm going to a place of execution. Come and go with me. Deny your own selfish ambitions and lust, and turn to me, and go to the Cross with me.'**

Idolatry takes many subtle ways in our lives. Even our pets can become idols. I've read about a pet the other day – a dog that inherited over a million dollars. That's the fact. You read that all the time. People leave their big estates to dogs and cats. You know, I love dogs. I've got three of them. Pardon me, they've got me. I love them. I've always loved cats. I was raised on a little dairy farm we've had to have cats to keep the rats down. If you wanna get rid of rats, get some cats. And you know we had a cat that lived for about 18 or 20 years and we never saw any rats. When that cat died, the rats and the mice where just about taking over and I told my wife as she's in the hospital, and I said, *'Darling, we've got to get us a cat.'* I said, *'The mice are everywhere.'*

We lived back up in the mountains about a mile from our nearest neighbour and I guess they come in from- I don't know where they come from. But from the woods and they even get in the trunk of a car. We can't even find where they nest. We've taken it to the garage. But there they are. You open the trunk lid and there are the rats. Come and see us sometime. Bring your helicopters. We'll spray them.(laughter)

Now Paul taught that a Christian is someone who is turned to God from idols to serve the living and the true God. There is a film showing throughout the world called 'The Idol Maker', but a Christian is an idol breaker.

And regardless of their decision Joshua said that **for me and my house we are going to serve the Lord.**

You know, Adam and Eve had to make a choice in the Garden of Eden. God said if you want to build a wonderful world, we'll build it together. But I'm going to test you, because I've given to you the ability to choose. I haven't made you a robot in which I can punch a button and you would obey me. I've made you in my image. You have the right to choose. So when Adam and Eve faced that choice they chose wrongly. They broke the law of God. And God said **"in the day that you do you will suffer and die".**

And mankind has been suffering ever since. And it all because of that first sin in the Garden of Eden. And man has been inheriting that tendency to sin ever since. The seed of sin is in us when we are born. David said, **'In sin did my mother conceive me.'** At conception sin was already planted. And then comes the age of accountability – moral accountability at about 9 or 10 years of age - when you are held accountable by God for your actions and you choose to sin. And then the rest of your life you practice sin. You are born towards sin, you choose to sin at a certain point and then you practice sin.

And the Bible says, **'We have all sinned'** and we are all idolatrous. Now Adam had to make a choice and he made the wrong choice. You have to make a choice. And then many choices like the rich young ruler. Remember he came to Jesus and he was filled with questions and he wanted eternal life, and he said, **'Sir, what must I do to find eternal life?'** Jesus said,–looked at him and loved him – said, **'Go sell all that you have. Give it to the poor. Take up the Cross. Follow me.'**

The young man was grieved. He wept. He wanted Christ, but he wanted his money more. Now if he had said, **'All right, I'll do it, Lord.'** I'm sure Lord would have said, **'No, it's not your money I want. I want your heart.'** It's our attitude towards these idols and towards these things. The television itself can become an idol. When we walk into the room all conversation stops and we sort of sit there in reverence watching that box to see if JR is gonna be shot again. (laughter)

I read the other day that Mary Martin who is mother in real life say that people now ask her to sign not her name Mary Martin, but JR's mother.

Now the Bible says we must choose between two ways of life. Jeremiah had written ***Thus says the LORD: Behold, I set before you the way of life and the way of death.*** There is a way of life; there is a way of death. Which way are you on? You must choose tonight. I read where *Alvin* Toffler indicated recently that for too many there simply is no way out for our modern world. No exit from the human dilemma as Jean Paul-Sartre once wrote. The scientists say, **'Invent your way out.'** The philosophers say, **'Think you way out.'** The sensualists say, **'Play your way out.'** But none of it works.

A month ago a twenty-six year old playboy killed himself because life had nothing else to offer him. And some are looking to the past for their way. So Barbra

Streisand signs 'The Way We Were'. O George Harrison and the Beatles used to sing 'Something in the Way'. But there is another song out there that says, 'Show Me the Way'. Jesus said, **'I am the one. I'm the only one. I'm the only way to permanent peace. I'm the only way to permanent joy. I'm the only way to eternal life. I'm the only way to forgiveness of sin. I'm the only way to the Father. You have to come by me.'**

And that eliminates a lot of people. When Jesus began to talk about dying on the Cross a lot of His followers left Him. They said, *'Lord, we thought you were gonna sit up on a big throne and we were gonna drive in Cadillacs, and we were gonna have beautiful swimming-pools, and lovely ladies, and all the rest of it. We didn't really know that you were going to die and wanted us to go with you. We thought this was going to be a kingdom and we were gonna overthrow Rome, and were gonna to rule the world.'*

And that is going to happen someday, but not now. The Cross before the Crown. Some of us want the

Crown before the Cross. The Bible says **'There is a *way* that seemeth right unto a man, *but the end* thereof are the *ways of death*.'** What are some other ways? Well some people say, *'I'm gonna follow my conscious.'* But you don't follow your conscious. Many of us have dead consciousness. You conscious is no longer a safe guide. You've hardened it, you've deadened it. And then other people say, *'Well I've tried to be sincere in everything I do.'* We are here on a football stadium right here; and many years ago I saw a man pick up a football and he ran 65 yards the wrong way. Now he was one of the most sincere fellas you ever saw. (laughter)Lost the game.

And then there are many people that say, *'Well you know, I do a lot of good works and I give money to charitable causes, and I do all that. I'm sure God will understand.'* The Bible says, **'For by grace are ye saved through faith; and that not of yourselves: but it is the gift of God:*Not of works, lest any man should boast.'*** See if you can work your way to Heaven and pay your way to Haven, you'd get up and say, *'Look what I did. I've got myself here by my own good works.'*

They only way you are ever going to make it is to come to the Cross. For Christ took our sins and our judgment, and our Hell, and identify yourself with Him. And then there are some people who say, *'Well I'll reform. I'll do better.'* I know people that are always saying *'I'm going to do better.'* But they never do better. They don't have any power within them to do better until they come to Christ. And when you come to Christ an explosion takes place of power that he gives you to live your life. I can't live the Christian life. I have no power within me to live the Christian life. The Holy Spirit has to live in me and Christ has to live through me. I cannot live the Christian life. I'm a total flop and failure.

Jesus said, **'Enter ye in at the strait gate: for wide is the gate, and broad is the way, that leadeth to destruction, many there be which go in there. Because strait is the gate, and narrow is the way, which leadeth unto life, and few there be that find it.'** He said only a few were going to find it. That narrow gate and that narrow way as I've said last evening. Are you among that few? You not only choose between two ways of life, but you choose between two masters. Jesus said, **'No man can serve two masters. For either he will love the one and hate the other or else he will hold to the one and despise the other. You cannot serve God and materialism'**, he says in Matthew the 6th chapter, the sermon on the mount. You have to make a choice. All the way through the Bible choices, choices, choices... Not only between two ways of life and two masters, but you are gonna have to choose between two fathers – two spiritual fathers. He said in John 8:44 a very shocking statement. He said, **'Ye are of your *father* the *devil,* and the *lusts* of *your father* ye *will do.*'**

He says for many of you the devil is your spiritual father. Now you are not aware of it, you wouldn't admit it, but that's the way God looks at it. There is either God, your spiritual father – the true and the living God, Christ, or there is the devil. I didn't say that, Jesus said it. Read the whole 8th chapter of John and you'll find out. Many say that they don't believe in the devil – I'm gonna talk about that one evening. But the last few years that's all changed. We've had 'The Exorcist' 'The Omen' and many other films along that line. And a few weeks ago there was a murder trial and the defense lawyers were arguing that the devil made their clients kill. And seventy some percent of the American people according to a poll taken a few months ago now say they believe in the devil. Well now if you don't have the devil, there is something stirring the world up to some sort of madness. Give him another name if you want to call him something else. Call him that. Call him the deceiver, the force, whatever you wanna call him.

Something's wrong. Something is causing lust and greed, and hate, and prejudice, and war, and murders, and rapings, and muggings. Who's causing all that? It's worldwide. It's the devil according to the Bible. Now if you don't wanna accept what the Bible says give it another name. Go to Star Wars and say it's the force of evil. It's there. And then you have to choose not only between two ways of life and two masters, and two fathers, but you have to choose between two destinies: Heaven or Hell.

Solomon wrote about the way to Hell in proverb 7:27. C.S. Lewis the great Cambridge and Oxford professor – he taught at both universities – used to emphasize, he said, *'No one ever had ever so much to say about the way to Hell as did Jesus Christ.'* And the youth of our days seems sometimes to be obsessed with the fact of Hell. You know, I used to take a little book and I would read the lyrics. That's back when Franklin, my son and my other children were going through that stage and my wife and I tried to keep up with them.

The loud noise was coming from their room and what they were listening to. And constantly you hear a song today called 'Highway to Hell'. The Meat Loaf sing 'Bat out of Hell'. And the AC/DC sing 'Hells Bells'. And there is a group in England that is singing at the top of the charts right now called The Damned. So you see, young people talk about it. They think about it.

On the other hand, no one ever spoke of Heaven with more clarity and authority as Jesus Christ. And one of the most played pop songs is Led Zeppelin's 'Stairway to Heaven'. Jesus Christ is the stairway to Heaven. He is the way to Heaven. Come to Him. He said, 'In my Father's house are many mansions if it were not so I would have told you.' Yes, Jesus is in Heaven preparing your estate right now. Waiting for you. There is a future life. And eternal life does not begin when you die and go to Heaven; it begins here and now when you make this choice for Christ. Because eternal life comes to dwell in your heart tonight. Jesus Christ is the gateway to Heaven.

Now this choice also you must make yourself. Joshua said, 'As for me and my house we will serve the Lord.' Your father can't make it for you. Your mothercan't make it for you. Your children can't make it for you. This is where you must choose yourself. He knew that he could not choose for the tribes of Israel. They must choose for themselves. Man is a social being. However, there is an inner sanctuary within ourselves where we retire from all other fellowships, comradeships and influences, and there is a lonely arena where the greatest battles of life must be fought alone.

And this is a decision that you have to make alone. You're asked to cast a vote. And you go in and you pull the string and the curtain pulls around you, and you vote for Christ or for the other gods. Which has your priority? That's the great question. Moses said, 'I call Heaven and Earth to record this day that I have set before you life and death, blessing and cursing: therefore choose life, that both thou and thy seed may live forever.' Notice that it says thy seed – this has something to do with your children and you grandchildren, and you children's children. My son and I were talking tonight about how it passes on from generation to generation – this faith that we have in Christ.

The writer of Hebrews recounts how Moses esteeming the reproach of Christ greater riches; chose rather to suffer the affliction with the people of God rather than enjoy the pleasures of sin. He made a choice. Moses could have probably been the Pharaoh of Egypt. He was a son of Pharaoh's daughter, heir to all the riches and power of Egypt. And he made a choice to suffer prosecution and the reproach with the people of God.

He didn't know that his name would be in history. He didn't know that someday he would lead all of Israel. He didn't know that someday he would be considered one of the greatest men that have ever lived. But he made that choice. He made it on the basis of simple faith in God. Some think that Guy Lafleur is the world's greatest hockey player. And he said a month ago that each of us has only one past, but there are many futures. You see, you can't change your past. But you can determine your destiny by deciding for Christ. And when you do that Christ changes your past. He wipes out all the sins of the past. Becauseyou see, the blood of Jesus Christ, His Son, cleanses from all sins.

Without the shading of blood there is no forgiveness. When He died on that Cross he forgave all the past. You tonight are reminded of the many sins in your life. The Holy Spirits bring them to your mind right now. And you know they stand against you at the judgment where every secret thing will be brought out. But Jesus tonight offers forgiveness. But he offers more than forgiveness, he offers justification: just as though you have never committed a sin. What a wonderful thing to go to bed tonight and to know that the past is gone, forgiven, cleansed. And God no longer remembers your sins.

Yes, and this choice is very urgent. To delay makes the right decision harder. Indecision is itself a choice. Not to decide is to decide not to.

Choose now.

Nowhere in the Bible does it promise a tomorrow. Come while you can. Time itself makes the decision for you if you don't. You say, *'But what do I have to do?'* Three things. You must be willing to repent of your sin; that means to change you way of thinking about you sins and realize how bad they are in the sight of God. Change your way of thinking about God and say, *'I love him and I'm going to love him with all my heart, mind and soul. I'm going to make Him the priority of my life. I'm going to put Him first from now on and He's going to be not only my savior, but my Lord.'* You may be a member of a church. You might not be a member of any church. You may be an officer in the church. But you are not sure about your relationship with Christ and you want to be sure.

And you must be willing to repent and secondly by faith, receive Christ into your heart that makes you put it all down here and trust Him and Him alone. And thirdly you follow and serve Him as His Disciple and follower, and obey Him. That means a big change for you if you make this choice. I'm going to ask you to make it now.

And I'm going to ask you to do it publicly as we've seen thousands of people this week already come to Cross. I'm going to ask you to get up from your seat if you start from the top stand there it will take you two minutes so start now. And come and stand in front of this platform as you all stand here in front of the platform I'm going to say a word to you and have a payer with you and then you can go back and join your friends. You are making that choice by coming and standing here.

And the reason I do it publicly is because every person that Jesus called, He called publicly. Joshua called upon the people publicly. Moses called upon the people publicly to inscribe their commitment that would be seen publicly for generations to come. I'm asking you tonight to publicly and openly come and say, *'Tonight Christ is going to be priority in my life. I want to know that I have eternal life.'* You may be in the choir, you may be sitting here on the grass, you may be sitting over there on the grass or in the stands. Wherever you are you come. We are going to wait for you. Quickly. Right now, as the choir sings softly. I'm going to ask that no one leave the stadium, please. It disturbs so many people that are on their way. Men, women, young people, God has spoken to you tonight. You come.

Chapter 5 - Who is Jesus?

1971 Chicago, Illinois

I'm going to ask that we all bow our heads in prayer. Every head bowed and every eye closed. For many thousands of people here today this will be an hour of decision and you will never be the same today. Even if you refuse Christ, you'll never be the same. Once you've faced Him, once you've heard the Gospel and rejected it, you can never be the same. It says when the rich young ruler rejected Christ, he turned away grieved, emotionally disturbed, because when you reject the claims of Christ that's a very serious thing. It will be an hour of decision for many of you who receive him today. Your life will never be the same; your home will never be the same. So let's listen carefully and prayerfully and reverently to the message of the word of God. Shall we pray...

'Our Father, we thank thee for this love of God that reaches around the world and engulfs all of

mankind. Thou does loves the Russians and the Chinese as much as thou loves the British or the Americans, or the Africans. Thou loves the whole world. And thou sent thy son to die for the whole world. And we are all included in thy redemption plan. And we thank thee that at this hour of history we can stand and proclaim good news. That God is love. And that God is willing to forgive. We pray that many this day will receive that message, accept it and act on it and live by it. For we ask it in His Name. Amen.'

We've been having a marvellous time here in Chicago. I think Cliff has already told you how big this building is. There is no indoor arena in the world except the Astrodome in Houston, Texas that's bigger than this. And here today thousands of people just about filled to capacity today.

Now today I want you to turn with me to Luke's Gospel the 11th chapter beginning with verse 29, I hope you have your Bibles. How many have a Bible today? Lift them up. Look at the Bibles. Thousands of Bibles everywhere. Now the 11th chapter and the 29th verse of Luke's Gospel. **'And when the people were gathered thick together, He began to say, This is an evil generation: they seek a sign; and there shall no sign be given it, but the sign of Jonas the prophet. For as Jonas was a sign unto the Ninevites, so shall also the Son of man be to this generation. The queen of the south shall rise up in the judgment with the men of this generation, and condemn them: for she came from the utmost parts of the earth to hear the Wisdom of Solomon; and, behold, a greater than Solomon is here. The men of Ninevah shall rise up in the judgment with this generation, and shall condemn it: for they repented at the preaching of Jonas; and, behold, a greater than Jonas is here.'**

Now ancient Israel wanted Jesus to do something sensational to prove that He was really the Son of God. But Jesus is saying in this passage **'You are seeking for a sign. All right, I'll give you a sign. I am the sign.'**

And Jesus was saying that the people of Jonas' day listened to the message of God and repented and they are going to rise up at the Judgment as witnesses against the people of Jesus' day that rejected Him. He said the queen of the south recognized the Wisdom of Solomon, but he said, **'In me you have a greater wisdom than all the Wisdom of Solomon.'** He said, **'You are blind. You cannot see the truth. You are deaf and you cannot hear the truth.'** He said, **'I'm the truth. I'm the light of the world. I'm the sign.'**

Now when you face Jesus what is your reaction? When you are confronted with Jesus Christ what is your reaction? The reaction of the Scribes and the Pharisees was one of hostility. The people of Nineveh's days were humbled and repented when they faced and confronted God. And the question that we all ask today is this question, "what think ye of Christ?'

There is a rock opera at the moment called 'Jesus Christ the Superstar'. All over the country thousands of young people are talking about Christ. They can't escape

Him. There is Broadway play right now entitled 'Godspell' – a musical version of St. Matthew's Gospel. There is a new movie right now called 'Brother John' in which Sidney Poitier plays Jesus Christ in the form of an Alabama black man. The front cover of LIFE magazine a few weeks ago ran 'Jesus Christ Superstar'. And this rock opera from England is confronting young people with one question – Who is Jesus Christ? An 87 minute long electronic probe into the life of Jesus.

Who is Jesus? And the opera concludes with the voice of Judas coming back from the dead and still questioning who Jesus is. *'Don't get me wrong'*, says Judas in the opera, *'I only want to know.'* Andthen the haunting chorus follows *'Jesus Christ Superstar, do you think you are what they say you are?'*

It's interesting to me that in 1971 the plays, the books, the operas, the movies are about Jesus. Our generation cannot escape Jesus and when good news for modern men come out, a new translation of the New Testament by the American Bible Society they sold 25 million copies. We cannot escape Jesus. I've never heard of an opera or a play even about Buddha or Mohammed, or Gandhi. But our generation has become hung up on Jesus. Young people are talking about Jesus. He's the subject of conversation today on the campus, in the high schools, everywhere. Young people are discussing Jesus Christ and they are asking the question *'Who is He? Who is this Jesus?'* We cannot escape Him.

You remember that day when Saul who was persecuting Christians was on the road to Damascus and a blinding light came and he felt down and the first question he asked was **'Who art thy Lord?'** The question that our generation of young people on the campus are asking today is *'Who art thy Lord?'* Who is Jesus? Why cannot we escape Him? Why is he in our conscience and in our mind so that our plays and our poems, and our operas are about Him? Is he just a revolutionary hero? Or is he something more? He only lived 33 years. He never traveled more than a hundred miles. He never had any formal education. And yet 2,000 years later an entire generation is talking about Jesus Christ.

Some say that he was a madman. Some of the people of his day said that he was mad, said he was a maniac. Was he? There were others that said he was a revolutionary. He'd come to lead a revolution. Was he a revolutionary? In the sense that he changed men's lives he was, but he never led a revolution against Rome. He never led a revolution against the existing authorities. As a matter of fact, some of them tried to get Him to and some of them thought He was going to. And when they found out that He was building a spiritual kingdom, they were no longer interested in Him. And when they tried to tempt Him about that he said, **'Bring me a coin.'** And He said, **'Whose picture's on that coin?'** They said, *'Caesar.'* He said, 'All right, render to Caesar the things that are Caesars and to God the things that are God's.' And the scripture says they quit asking Him questions. They didn't know how to answer that.

Or was Jesus an establishment man? Some people say that he represented the status quo. Some people say that Jesus Christ is the one upon which western culture has been built and that America is really Jesus' organization on Earth. But I wanna tell you if His organization depends on the bureaucracy we build up in Washington, we are finished. There is not much hope for the world. Jesus Christ is not the establishment Christ. He's building another kingdom. He's building an eternal kingdom.

And then there are some people that say that he was the first hippie. They say that He had long hair, went around with His disciples in a commune. You know, actually we don't know what He looked like. We don't know whether He had a long beard or not. Those are just pictures that artists have painted. We think He did.We don't know whether He had long hair or not. He probably did, because the people of that day say that was the style. But we don't know. We don't have a picture of Jesus and God did that purposefully. So that we would not be worshipping an image. Because God is a spirit and must be worshipped in spirit.

And then there were people that said that He was deliberately evil. That He was an evil man. That He was a devil. What was He?! That's the question. Jesus Christ who are You? Who is Jesus? We can't escape Him. We try to run from Him but there He is. He keeps popping up everywhere. Our greatest philosophers write about Him. Our greatest historians write about Him. Our greatest poems and plays are about Him. Our greatest architectures are about Him even in the Soviet Union - you go to the Kremlin. I've been in the Kremlin and it's all filled about Jesus. You go anywhere in the Soviet Union and you'll see images and art, and much of the music has to do with Jesus. They can't escape Him.

Well we know some things about Him. We know He was a man. Jesus was completely human. He was representative of men, because the bible says **He was identified, He was numbered with the transgressors.** We know that He was hungry. We know He got thirsty.

We know He got tired. We know that he had the joys of friendship. We know that He wept at the tomb of a dead loved one. We know that He had all the characteristics of a man and yet very interestingly the Bible says that He never committed a sin. In fact, He stood in front of the people of His generation and said, **'I've never committed a sin.'** He said, **'have any of you my neighbors have ever seen me commit a sin?'** They couldn't say a thing. And wouldn't that be something for a man to come along 33 years of age and say who of you have ever seen me commit a sin? I tell you if I'd say that all my team will jump straight up and say, *'I have.'* My wife's here. All of us are sinners, but Jesus was tempted in every point; like as we are. He went through every temptation you've ever been through. There isn't a trial or a testing, or a temptation that Jesus has not been through before you and he resisted them, and overcame them all. Every one, He was a man. Just like you. But He was more than that.

He claimed to be the unique only begotten incarnate Son of God. In fact, He claimed pre-existence. The scripture says, **'In the beginning was the word. And the word was with God.'** Before time began he existed. He said, **'Before Abraham was, I am in eternal existence.'** No wonder they got angry. No wonder they threw stones at him. No wonder they tried to kill Him. No wonder they eventually did crucify Him. He stood and said, **'I am God.'** Was He? Was He who He claimed to be? The Son of the living God?

One day He asked His disciples **'Who do men say that I am?'** And Peter answered and said, **'Well, some say you are John the Baptist come back, or you are a Jeremiah or you are Elijah.'** He said, **'I'm really not interested in what the people say. I'm interested Peter in what you say. What do you say?'** Peter said **'Thou art the Christ, the Son of the living God.'** And Jesus said, **'Peter, you've done well. You've passed your examination. But Peter those are not your thoughts,**

those thoughts came from God. It has been revealed to you by God.'

Jesus Christ claimed to be the Son of the living God. And you know at His incarnation or His birth that was not His birth, or that wasn't the beginning, that wasn't the origin of Jesus. That was the beginning of His incarnation. Because He has always existed from everlasting to everlasting; He's God the Bible says. And the word was made flesh and dwelt among us. In other words, *the Logos*, the word of God, the eternal God became flesh in the person of Jesus Christ and lived like a man among us. That's what the Bible teaches and when you come to Jesus Christ you have to accept that.

He wasn't just another revolutionary. He wasn't just another hippie. He was not just another great man. He was God in the flesh. And all the ethics that He taught. Never a man spoke like that Man. **'When you get hit on one side,'** he said, **'turn the other cheek.'** He never said what to do after that. But He did say forgive seventy times seven; count that out. How about the little irritations from your wife? Or your husband. Seventy times seven you forgive. My wife once said that the secret of a happy marriage is two good forgivers. And that's what it is. Two good forgivers. People that can forgive each other.

Jesus taught that we are to forgive. He taught a revolution in the way we are to live. He taught us that it wasn't just our outward actions that God judges, but the inward thoughts and intents. He said, Moses said in the Ten Commandments **'Thou shall not commit adultery'**, but I tell you that if you look on a woman to lust after her, you've already committed it. He said, Moses said, **'Thou shall not murder.'** But I tell you if you have hate in your heart against your brother without cause you are already guilty.

He lifted men's ethics to the highest plain and demanded that we live that kind of a life. He himself lived that kind of a life. And the scripture says that he judges the inside. The Attorney General of the United States said the other day that America is imperiled more from within than without. And so are you here today, in your personal life. David said, **'In sin did my mother conceive me.'** Jesus said, **'Out of the heart perceive evil thoughts and murders, and adulteress, and thefts, and blasphemies.'** All the evil in the world comes from the human heart. That's got to be changed. And that's why Jesus said, **'You must be born again. You must be converted. You must have a new beginning.'** And He can do it.

How do you explain Jesus? Jesus Christ, are You what You say You are? You know, they only brought three charges against Him, to crucify Him. One, they said, **'This man love sinners.'** That was one charge. The second — **He healed on the Sabbath day.** And the third — **He claimed to be the Son of God.** Was He the Son of God? Look at His authority. Jesus came unto them saying **'All authority has been given to me.'** I know one thing; He forgave sin and no prophet ever did that. Jesus Himself forgave sin. He said, **'Thy sins are forgiven thee.'**

And nobody had authority over nature. One night He was in a storm. The lightning was flashing, the thunder was roaring, the sea was raging, the wind was blowing, the disciples were afraid and Jesus was asleep in the boat, and He stood up in the boat and said, **'Please, be still.'** The lightning quit its flashing and the thunder quit it roaring, and the rain ceased to fall, and the wind quieted down, and the sea quieted down, and nature obeyed Him. And our young people believe that today, because one of their top tunes at the moment is *'Put your hand in the hand / Of the One who calmed the sea'*. He calmed the sea. He had power over nature.

I was flying, Cliff Barrows and some of us were flying some time ago. I think we were in a typhoon leaving the Philippines. And just before we got out of the typhoon the captain of the plane had invited me to sit up front with him. And it was fairly smooth. We had a lot of rain and all but it wasn't too rough. But all of a sudden the plane hit something; it seemed to me as though it hit a wall. It jolted and jerked and quivered, and went up and down for about two minutes and then all of a sudden we plunged out into brilliant sunshine and the smooth air. And the captain turned to me with the perspiration running down his face and he said *'You know, that was God telling us there is something up here more powerful than this airplane.'*

But Jesus could take a storm like that and turn it around. He could take a lightning and throw it back in the cloud. He has power over nature. Why? Because He is the God of nature. Those are His laws, they are obeying Him. He had authority over disease. I read the other day where Mao Zedong in China claims to have cured 80% of all the deaf people in China. And one of those men that came back on the Ping-Pong team said that Mao Zedong is the Jesus Christ of China today. They talk about personality cult. Looks like to me they've got quite a personality over there. But Jesus did make the blind to see. He made the deaf to hear. He made the dumb to talk. He raised the dead. According to the record He had authority over demons.

You say, *'Billy, do you believe in demons?'* – *'I surely do.'* And Jesus confronted demons time after time and he could cast them out. And people that were insane under the powers of demons would regain their sanity. And then look at the death He died. Did ever a man die like Jesus? The lightning flashed and the thunder roared and then the earth began to shake. And even the soldiers confessed that this must be the Son of God. Anyone that can see Jesus on that Cross and not be touched has a heart of stone. They first took off His clothes. Then they took long leather thongs with steel pellets or lead pellets on the end and beat Him across the back until He could hardly stand up. Then they put a crown of thorns on His brow and His face was bleeding. And they laughed at Him. And they spit on Him. And they mocked Him.

And with one snap of His finger 72,000 angels had already drawn their swords ready come to their rescue and wipe this planet out of existence in the universe. And the Jesus said, **'No. To this end was I born.'** And he dragged and lifted, and hauled that Cross. And don't you ever forget one thing the man that helped Jesus carry that Cross was a black man. And don't ever forget another thing Jesus belongs to Africa as much as He does to Europe and Asia. He was born in that part of the world that touches Africa and Asia, and Europe. And Jesus was not a white man like me, nor was he as black as some of you.

We don't know the color of His skin, but it must have been a dark color like the people of His day, because He was a man like them. Don't ever say it's a white's man religion or a black man's religion. It's a world religion. He belongs to the world. (applause) When He died on that Cross and they nailed him, they put the nails in his hands, and you know what He said, **'Forgive them for they know not what they do.'**Could you forgive somebody that's putting nails in your hands and you know you didn't deserve it. He didn't yell, he didn't scream – He just took it. And said, **'Lord, forgive** them. **They don't know what they are doing.'** That's how He confronted the violence of His day.

And then on the Cross He said, **'My God, why have thou forsaken Me?'** And then He dropped His head and said, **'It's finished.'** What did He mean? He meant your plan of salvation was finished. God can now forgive you of all your sins, because Jesus had finished God's plan for your salvation. Because, you see, God knows every one of you by name. He has the hairs of your head numbered. God looks upon you as though you were the only person in the whole universe. He sees you and you alone. And on that cross Jesus had the capacity to think of you. And He loved you enough to stay on the Cross. Was there ever such love as that? When He could have been rescued and taken back to Heaven, and to sit on His throne, but He didn't. He said, **'No. I'm doing it for the joy that is set before me.'** Because He saw that He would be raised from the dead. He saw that there would be a gathering in the generations to come of a people for His name that would make up His body. He saw the day when we will reign with Him in His Kingdom.

Yes, they laid Him away in a tomb and that's where the Jesus Christ Superstar leaves it. But out in Kansas City they got a hold of the rock opera and they carried it right on to the next step – the Resurrection. And if you don't have the Resurrection – you don't have any Gospel. Jesus Christ is alive. And when they went out to the tomb that morning, they heard the greatest news the world has ever known. He is not here. He is risen. He is alive today. And the thing that inspired the Disciples to turn the world upside down in there day was the Resurrection. They went everywhere declaring that Jesus is alive.

You know, some of us Christians live as though Jesus is dead. He's not dead. He's alive. All of you are going through the troubles of your trials, and your temptations, and your testings, and your pressures. And you are under satanic attack all the time, constantly. You know, I think in many ways, in some ways it's easier not to be a Christian in this world, because the devil may leave you alone. The moment you receive Christ as savior you're in for it unless you live on your knees and live on your scriptures, and keep your guard up, and have your spiritual armor on at all times. Because if you let down even one day as a Christian, you are in trouble. The moment you receive Christ, you see, all the world is going this way – you turn around and start against the tide as a Christian. And that's hard.

But you know, it's hard to be a sinner too the older you get. Because the Bible says, **'The way of the transgressor is hard.'** I watch sometimes the programs on television where they have crime. I have never seen in my life seen criminals work so hard for the money they get. It looks like to me they could get a legitimate business and have a much easier time to get their money. They work at it. That is according to the script. And I'm sure they do in real life.

Jesus Christ is alive. And if He's not risen from the dead, if He's not alive then there is no such thing as

Christianity; we're yet in our sins as Paul said – forget it. And then the people that never received Christ – what has happened to them? We had a fella here the other night that was a Black Panther leader. He said that he thought he could change the world through the Black Panther movement, until he said, he met Jesus. And he said Jesus changed his life, and took all the hate out. And now he said, 'I believe the world can be changed. But I believe it can be done with Jesus' power.' That's it – Jesus coming into our heart.

You know, if I had no proof whatsoever, no scientific proof that Jesus ever lived I still would trust Him, because of what He's done for me. The joy and the peace, and the security, and the love that He's given to me; His grace that is mine today. And then the satisfaction that he gives to those who have trusted Him. **Who are thou, Lord?** Jesus Christ, are You who You say You are. This is the question thatevery one of you today are going to have to answer. Who is Jesus? If Jesus claimed to be God knowing He wasn't God then He's a liar. And we will have to say, 'Jesus, you are a liar. You are a fraud and a hoax, and you're the biggest fraud in the history of the human race; or if Jesus thought He was God and did not know the difference then He desperately needed mental help, he needed several psychiatrists.

The third alternative is that He was who He claims to be – God in the flesh. I believe that the evidence is overwhelming that He is who He claims to be – the Son of the living God. But I cannot prove it scientifically. But I can prove it by the lives that He transforms every day. I can prove it, because in my heart I don't say, 'I think' or 'I hope', I say, 'I know.'

And you know, there is another element in our lives that we don't think much about and that's the element of faith. You think of the faith that you have to have every day. You have to have faith that your wife didn't put poison in your coffee this morning. You have to have faith in her. She might have felt like it, but she didn't. (laughter) You have to have faith in the bank when you write a check and sign it. You have to have faith in the bank. You have to have faith that the bank is gonna pay it. You have to have faith in the government. When you pull out a dollar bill and I know it's shrinking, but you have to have faith that it is a dollar. That people will accept it as money. Everything we do is by faith.

Now for example, when I come up on a hill - and I live in the mountains of North Carolina, and we have a lot of hills – I don't stop my car before I get to the crest of the hill and get out and walk over, and see if somebody is coming up the other side on the wrong side, I have faith that the drivers are gonna stay on their side. FAITH, FAITH, FAITH. Everything. When you sat in that chair, have you sat in that chair before? I bet you didn't pick it up and examine it, and put your hands on it to see if it would hold you. By faith you just sat down in it. You had faith that people wouldn't build a chair that wouldn't hold you. Everything we do is by faith.

All right, take the same faith. Put it in Jesus Christ as your Lord and savior and you will know who Jesus is.

You accept Him by faith. And He comes into your life and into your heart, and you know that He is who He claims to be. (applause)

On that Damascus road that I referred to a moment ago the apostle Paul said, **'Who art thou Lord?'** And then Paul asked Him another question. Paul said, **'What do you want me to do, Lord?'** And Jesus said, **'Arise and go.'** I'm asking you today to arise and come to Him. Now some of you can ridicule. Some of you can reject Him. Some can just put it off and say, 'I'm gonna wait till another time.' Or you can accept Him as your Lord and your savior, and your Master, and the Son of God. And He will come into your heart, and forgive your sin, and change your life. Jesus Christ Superstar. **'Judas; don't get me wrong I only want to know'**, He said and then the haunting chorus *'Jesus Christ Superstar do You think You are what they say You are?'* – Yes. And more, ten thousand times more than two men in England ever put in those lyrics is Jesus Christ, The Son of God.

And you are asked today to receive Him. In fact, if you are going to go to Heaven the Bible teaches you have to receive Him; if you are going to have your sins forgiven, you have to receive Him. And I'm going to ask you to do it today. And I'm going to ask you to do it publicly. How do you do it? I'm going to ask hundreds of you to get up out of your seat right now and come, and stand in front of this platform quietly and reverently, and say, *'I want Christ in my heart. I want Him to forgive my sins. I want to know I'm going to Heaven. I want Him to change my life. I receive Him as my Lord and savior.'* If you are with friends or relatives, or in a delegation, they'll wait; if you've come in a bus, they'll wait. Why do I ask you to come forward?,- because every person Jesus ever called in the New Testament He called publicly. You come publicly and openly, and declare yourself.

You may be Protestant, you may be Catholic, you may be Jewish, you may be Orthodox or you may not have any religion. But God is spoken to you today and you know that you need Christ. You come and make sure right now. We are going to wait and I'm going to ask that no one leave the service, please; not at this holy moment. I know you want to go, because of the crowd, but don't leave. Just get up and come right now. Quickly. From everywhere. Hundreds of you. We are going to wait. From all over the stadium as God is speaking. You may be in the choir and this may be your last moment with God. You may never have another hour like this. You come.

Chapter 6 - The Offence of the Cross

1958 San Francisco, California

Tonight I want you to turn with me to 1st Corinthians the first chapter. All of you with your Bibles turn to 1st Corinthians the first chapter. And 1st Corinthians comes right before 2nd Corinthians if you have any difficulty finding it. How many have your Bibles? Lift them up. Wonderful. Thousands of people with Bibles. The first chapter of 1st Corinthians beginning with the 17th verse and tonight I want to speak of the subject 'The Offence of the Cross.' **For Christ did not send me to baptize, but to preach the gospel—not with wisdom and eloquence, lest the cross of Christ be emptied of its power.**

Paul said **'In my preaching that if I did it with cleverness and with the wisdom of words then with the Cross lose its effect.'** He said **'For the preaching of the Cross is to them that perish foolishness.'**

In other words Paul said that a sermon like I'm going to preach to you tonight is foolish to you that are perishing. It is a foolish subject. It will be a foolish message. The apostle said that 1900 years ago. For it is written: **'I will destroy the wisdom of the wise, and will bring to nothing the understanding of the prudent.'** Where is the wise; where is the disputer of this world? Has not God made foolish the wisdom of this world?

Look at the word wisdom today. Where is it? Our best brains are trying to build bigger and better bombs, more effective missiles and engines of destruction, Frankenstein monsters that can destroy civilization. All of our thoughts and intellectualism; all of our vaunted culture. The scripture says, **'God has made it foolish.--- For after that in the wisdom of God the world by wisdom knew not God, it pleased God by the foolishness of preaching to save them that believe.'** God has chosen this method to save men from destruction and judgment, and hell. You cannot come to Christ except you hear the Gospel. For the Jews require a sign and the Greeks seek after wisdom. But we preach Christ crucified unto the the Jews a stumbling block and unto the gentiles foolishness. But unto them which are called the Jews and Greeks in Christ, the power of God and the wisdom of God, because the foolishness of God is wiser than men.

This cross, this preaching of the Gospel of Jesus Christ the scripture says is wiser than all the men of all the ages; wiser than all the university professors; wiser than all the intellectuals. It's foolish to the world, but God says this very foolishness is wiser than this world. And the weakness of God – the Cross – seems to be to the world a weakness. The weakness of God is stronger than men. **But God hath chosen the foolish things of the world to confound the wise; and God hath chosen the weak things of the world to confound the things which are mighty; and the base things of the world and the despised God has chosen.**

Think about it. The Cross was a base thing. It was a thing to be despised. It was called a scandal among men. And yet God chose that method to confound the wise and to save the world. **That no flesh should glory in his presence.** No man will ever be able to stand in Heaven and say, *'I got here by my own ability, by my own works.'*

We will have to stand and say when we get to Heaven *'We got here by the Cross. We got here by the death of Christ on the Cross.'* And the fact that He was raised again from the dead. And I say as it has been said 2000 years before, **He was despised and rejected by men; a man of sorrows, and acquainted with grief.**

The Apostle Paul said in all of his preaching, in all of his proclaiming of the Gospel---**There is an offence to the Cross.** Paul said, **'I can preach anything else and there is no offence.'** But when you preach the Cross there is an offence. And this expression the Offence of the Cross sounds strange to our modern ears. Because you see, we have a beautiful Cross on our churches; we have crosses in the lapels of our coats; we have crosses around our necks, we have crosses embossed on our Bibles. We never think of it as a scandal and as an offence. And yet the Bible says it's a stumbling block. It's an offence; it's a scandal among men. It is an old rugged Cross. It was a place to execute criminals. It was a place where the violent died. And when I see Christ hanging on the Cross I say like Isaiah, *'There is no beauty that I should desire Him.'*

Paul says that in his day there was an offence and I found in my own ministry that I can preach anything else and it is called popular and pleases the ear; but when I come to the heart of Christianity, when I come to the cross and the blood in the resurrection that is the stumbling block, that's the thing people do not want to hear, that's the thing that is foolish. That's the thing that is an offence. And yet that is that very thing that is the heart of the Gospel. And without the Cross there is no salvation, there is no forgiveness. God said, **'I'll meet the human race only one place'**- that is the Cross. And if you havn't been to the Cross then there is no salvation and there is no forgiveness.

Why is the Cross an offence? I got thinking about this not long ago. Why the Cross is an offence? I see Christ hanging on the tree. I see Him dying for me. I see blood being shed. I see nails in his hands. I see a spike in his feet. And I see Christ dying for sin; an offence. Why is it an offence? First, the Cross is an offence, because it is the condemnation of the world. The Cross says to the world, **'You are sinner.'** The Cross said to the thief that was dying on the other cross, **'You are a sinner. You better repent.'** And the thief did repent. He confessed his sins and he said, **'Remember me when thou comest into thy kingdom.'** And Jesus turned to him and said, **'Today thou shalt be with me in Paradise.'** Christ forgave him right there, but first the Cross condemned his sins and made him confess and acknowledge that he was a sinner.

To the centurion who had helped nail him there. The Cross said to the centurion, **'You are a sinner.'** And the Centurion had to exclaim, **'Surely this must have been the Son of God!'**

The Cross said to Herod, **'You are an immoral man. You are living in adultery.'** And the Cross speaks to you about your sins tonight – your sins of immorality. There is no sin in the Bible that the Bible condemns more than the sin of immorality. It is America's great sin tonight. It is the same sin that caused destruction of Sodom and Gomorrah. It is a sin that God hates and God said, **'If they have ever looked on a person of the opposite sex with lust have committed it already.'** And Cross said to Herod **'You are living in immorality. And you are going to go to Hell for that unless you repent of sin.'** And Herod didn't like it. And Herod rebelled; he cringed under the impact of the Cross which became a conscious to Herod and spoke to Herod. And tonight some of you are cringing, because you know that that is your sin. Look at another man Caiaphas— proud, cold, crafty--- wise old man in his pride. And the Cross said to him, **'You are a sinner. You are a religious leader, but you are a sinner.'**

Jesus had said to Nicodemus **'Except a man be born again, he cannot see the kingdom of God.'** And I tell you I don't care if you are a Sunday school teacher, if you are a deacon or an elder, or a church leader unless there has been a personal encounter with the Lord Jesus Christ, it means nothing.

We have a lot of religiosity in this country. We have a great deal of religion in America. We have a great deal of worshipping in America that is not true worship.

The Pharisees – fasted twice a week, they were Orthodox; they were fundamental; they believed the scriptures from cover to cover. And yet Jesus in the most scathing language denounced them. And indicated they were not saved, and indicated they would come to Him on the last day and He would say, **'Depart from me you cursed. I never knew you.'**

Caiaphas was a religious leader and yet he helped crucify Jesus. Pride--- And there is no pride in all the world as terrible as religious pride. Proud of our religion; proud of the things we do – the externals of religion when we are filled with pride and jealousy and envy, and gossiping.

And we do not have love. **'By this all men will know that you are My disciples, if you have love for one another.'** Do we love? **'By their fruits ye shall know them.'** And the fruit of the Spirit is love, joy and peace. And if I see a person who isn't loving his brother in Christ, I have a right to doubt whether that man has ever been to the Cross no matter who he is or how much he says he believes; because the Bible says, **'The devils** believe.' Oh the devils are Orthodox. Believe and tremble.

Look at Pilate--- The Cross said to Pilate, **'Pilate, you are a coward. Pilate, you are a sinner.'** And Pilate didn't like it; he cringed and tried to run from the savior.

Look at Judas. The Cross says to Judas, **'Judas, you're covetous. And that is idolatry.'** Judas was with Jesus for three years. He had heard all the sermons that Jesus had preached and in fact Judas had baptized. Judas had been on Jesus' team; had travelled for three years with Christ; had been one of His intimate companions. And yet Judas was lost. Judas was covetous all the time. Judas was lost in the end, because he had never realized the personal intimate presence of Christ and he had never understood nor been to the Cross by faith. And had an encounter with Christ that counts, and it's possible to be in the organization that Christ founded. It's possible to be in all the religious organizations. And if Judas, who spent three years travelling with Jesus, was lost that should cause all of us to search our hearts. See how we stand.

The soldiers that gambled for his garment--- the Cross to all of these people says, **'You are sinner.'** And when Paul preached the Cross before governor Felix, he trembled and said, **'When I have a more convenient season, I will call for thee.'** Felix tried to get away. Why? Festus said to Paul when he preached the cross to him, he said, "you're mad Paul". Agrippa said "almost thou persuadest me to become a Christian." And the cross has come down through the centuries passing it's unfaltering judgment upon the vanities, prides, hates, greeds and self indulgent pleasures and lust of men. The Cross says to us all, **'You are a sinner.'** It becomes the conscience of the world, the Bible says, **'All have sinned and come short of the glory of God.'**

And when I come to the Cross the first thing I have to say is *'I am a sinner.'* But the scripture says, **'Men love darkness, because their deeds are evil.'** You don't want the light of the Cross. And so the Cross becomes a stumbling block. It becomes foolish to you. When you realize that you must give up your sins. When you realize that you must acknowledge that you are a sinner. You say, *'No, no!'* And you cringe and go back into your darkness. And the light of the Cross begins to penetrate into your extortion, into your pride, into your idolatry, into your bigotry, into your intolerance. Into all the sins of your life the Cross sends a beam of life and you cringe back and say, *'No, no, no. Don't expose me.'*

And the Cross goes down into the dark recesses of your heart where even your wife and husband cannot go, even your family cannot go, even your best friends cannot go - down deep inside of you and seizes the sins and exposes them to the light. And God says, **'Someday every secret thing shall be brought out.'** And the Cross says, **'You are a sinner in need of repentance.'** And so the Cross becomes a stumbling block and it's an offence to all of us that are sinners tonight; because we don't like to be told that we are sinners and we don't like to acknowledge that we've broken God's law. You see, we are all proud. We don't like to come to an old Cross where blood is being shed and say, *'Oh, God, I'm a sinner. Forgive me.'* We don't like to do that because we have to come in humility. One of the reasons I ask people to come forward in these crusades. It's not only an expression of their will, but it is also an expression of humility. Jesus could have healed the man with the withered arm by saying, *'Be healed.'* But He didn't do it. Jesus said, **'Stretch it forth.'** He wanted the man to do something.

When I ask people to come forward in a crusade, I'm asking them to do something, to express their will, to say, *'I will receive Christ. I will follow Him. I will serve Him. I will come to the Cross and acknowledge that I'm a sinner and turn from my sins.'* And then secondly, the Cross of Jesus Christ is an offence, because blood was shed there. We hear a great deal about the Slaughterhouse Religion - religion of blood. And some people don't like it. And it becomes an offence. But the Bible says, **'The life of the flesh is in the blood.'**

And the Bible says eight things about the blood of Jesus Christ. First, the Bible says, it is the blood of propitiation. Romans 3:25 **'Whom God hath set forth to be a propitiation through faith in his blood, to declare his righteousness for the forgiveness of sins that are**

past.' The word propitiation means mercy. It is a place where God covers our sins and I tell you that your sins will never be covered except by the shed blood of Jesus Christ.

Secondly, it is the blood of redemption. Revelation 5:9 **'And they sang a new song, saying, Thou art worthy to take the book, and to open the seals thereof: for thou wast slain, and hast redeemed us to God by thy blood out of every kindred, and tongue, and people, and nation.'** We are bought back by the blood of Christ. We were not bought with silver and gold, and the precious stones. God paid the price of the blood of His only Son who died on the Cross for our redemption. He could have given one of His planets. Scientists tell that He has billions of them. He could have given a planet. He could have given all the oil, all gold and all the silver in all the world, because it's all His. But He didn't do it. He came and shed the blood of His only Son on the Cross. And it becomes an offence because of the blood. But it's the only place that you can meet God. It's the only way you'll ever have forgiveness. If you want forgiveness of your sins and you want to go to Heaven, you have to come the way of the blood.

And then thirdly, it is the blood of remission. Hebrews 9:22 **'And all things are by the law purged with blood; and without the shedding of blood there is no forgiveness.'** The scripture says that without the shedding of blood there is no forgiveness. How can you get around that? You'd have to tear out half the Bible if you take the blood out of the Bible. It's there and it teaches that without the shedding of blood there is no forgiveness.

It is the blood of the reconciliation. Our sins have separated between ourselves and God. Ephesians 2: 13, 'But now in Christ Jesus ye who sometimes were far off are made nigh by the blood of Christ.' In other words, our sins have separated between us and God and the scripture says, "be ye reconciled to God". How can I get back to God?

There is an empty space in your life. Down deep inside of you there is a sense of not belonging, of incompleteness and you've been searching for joy and peace and calmness. You'll never find that fulfillment, you'll never find that completeness apart from the person of Jesus Christ and apart from God's fellowship, because you were made in the image of God, made for fellowship with God and without God there is no joy and peace deep down in your soul. And the only way that you can be reconciled to God, the scripture says is by the blood that was shed on that Cross.

It is also the blood of justification. Romans 5:9 **'Justified by his blood, we shall be saved from wrath through him.'** Justified? Justification means a lot more than forgiveness. Forgiveness is not enough – I must be justified, just as if I have never sinned; just as though I have never committed one sin. God wipes out the past. He forgets my sins. He puts my sins in the depths of the sea. How and why? **Justified by His blood.**

Then it's the blood of peace. Colossians 1:20 **'We have peace through the blood of His Cross.'** You've been searching for peace, haven't you? You want joy and peace in your heart. You want peace with God, peace with your neighbors and peace deep down inside.

Everywhere you've searched: you've gone to the psychiatrist; you've read all the books that you could find that had the title 'peace'. All right, I'm going to tell you how you can get peace. And I don't believe there is any permanent peace outside of this – you can get peace at the Cross and only there.

And then seventhly, it is the blood of entrance Hebrews 10:19 **'Having therefore, brethren, boldness to enter into the holiest by the blood of Christ.'** And when I come into God's presence I don't come as a Pharisee and say, **'God, I thank thee, that I am not as other men are.'***"Lord I've preached to crowds of people. Lord I'm a fairly good man. I try to be decent. I try to tell the truth. I try to treat my neighbors as myself. I try to do all of these things. And Lord, I deserve to be in Heaven.'* No! He would reject me. When I stand in the judgment in that day I shall plead only one thing; the fact that one day by faith I went to the Cross and gave my life to Jesus, and had my sins cleaned by His blood. That is my only claim to Heaven. I don't claim to be going to Heaven today because I have preached or because I'm a good man. I claim to be going to Heaven only on the merit and the ground of Jesus and His death on the cross.

And then it is the blood that cleanses John 1:6 **'The blood of Jesus Christ his Son cleanseth us from all sin.'** Martin Luther was once reminded by the Devil of his many sins and he tabulated them. *'Is that all?'*, asked Luther. *'No there are many-many more'*, sneered Satan and added many more. *'Is that all?'* – *'Yes'*, said the Devil – *'Now, write beneath them all---***The blood of Jesus Christ his Son cleanseth us from all sin.**

J.P.Morgan's will contained ten thousand words--- he made many transactions and some of them affected the entire financial equilibrium of the world. Here is what J.P.Morgan put in his will to his children: '*I commit my soul into the hands of my Savior, full of confidence that having redeemed me and washed me in His most precious blood He will present me faultless before the throne of my Heavenly Father, and I entreat my children to maintain and defend, at all hazard, and at all cost of personal sacrifice, the blessed doctrine of* *complete atonement of sins through the blood of Jesus Christ, once offered, and through that alone.'*

J.P.Morgan was right and J. P. Morgan is in Heaven tonight not because he was a great financier, not because he was a great philanthropist, but because he was trusting in the atonement of Jesus Christ.

You say, *'But what does the blood mean?'* The Bible says, **'The life of the flesh is in the blood.'** The word blood means the life – the life of Christ given on the Cross. The word blood is symbolic in the Bible of life. He gave his life. He emptied Himself for us on the Cross. He took our sins by emptying Himself, by taking our suffering, and our sin, and our Hell. There is much mystery to the Cross. There are many things about the Cross that I don't understand, but there is this one thing that I know – it is the way of salvation. And I'm to come by faith even though it may seem foolish and irrational, and it may not seem the right thing to do and people may laugh at it. Yet, God says He's chosen the preaching of the Cross to bring men to Himself.

And then thirdly, the Cross of Christ is an offence, because it sets forth an imperative ideal of life. Jesus said, **'If anyone would come after me, let him deny himself and take up his cross and follow me.'** Christ demands that when you come to the Cross that you take up a cross. And we don't like that. That is an offence. That is a stumbling block. It's not a matter of just coming to the Cross one time or two times, or ten times. It's not the matter of leaving the Cross, but sharing Christ's rejection – taking up your own cross. Christ demands that we live a life of self-crucifixion. We refuse to give up what we know the Cross condemns. It might be not be popular to take a stand on a moral issue. It means that you take your stand against intolerance and bigotry. It means that you take your stand on social issues in your community that may not be popular. That's not easy to do. Even on the campus. It means that you take a stand for Jesus Christ even if they sneer and laugh, and mock, and ridicule. It means that you share the rejection of Jesus Christ. It means that you as a businessman go back to your business and put into your business Christian principles no matter what it may cost you financially. That's what it means.

And Jesus said that unless you are willing to take up the Cross and follow Him, you cannot be His disciple. Are you willing to take up the Cross? It means that you are going to have to forgive your husband or your wife who you've been quarrelling with. It means you are going to have to forgive that man that did something against you. It means that you are going to start a whole new realm of life. That is the Crucifixion Christ is talking about. That is the Cross. Are you willing to bear it? It will mean opposition. In fact, Jesus listed several types of opposition. He said, **'First there will be civic opposition – they will deliver you up before the councils.'** He said, **'There may be national opposition – you shall be brought before governors and kings for My sake.'** There might even be ecclesiastical opposition, because he said they will scourge you in their churches.

When Lord Shaftesbury tried to get through a Bill to ease the working conditions of the laboring people in England and to end the child labor in England that was crushing the youth of England, almost every bishop in the church opposed him. Yet he stood his ground and won the battle. And every bishop in 1958 would agree that Shaftesbury was right; it cost him something.

In 1861 when they were talking about ending slavery one of the major denominations of this country said, *'It's the church's duty to preserve slavery.'* And those that were against slavery were crucified even within the church. It also may mean domestic opposition. Jesus said a man's foes will be those of his own household; that there might be people in your own house who will not understand and think that you've gone crazy. They will be ready to take you to the psychiatrist if you really give your life to Christ. Because, you see, Christ will be so foreign to them when you start reading your Bible and praying, and going to church – it may mean opposition within your own household. But you must take your stand. Do it courteously and lovingly but take your stand.

And then it may mean opposition in general. And the Christian life is not easy. Don't let anybody tell you that it is easy. Jesus said take my yoke, "It is light" and thanks be unto God that there is joy and peace in the midst of crucifixion. There is joy and peace when the nails are going in the hands. But there may be suffering in living for Jesus and you must be willing to face it. That's the cost of discipleship. Are you ready to take up your cross?

And then lastly, the Cross of Christ is an offence, because it claims to be the power of God unto salvation. And it makes this claim without an alternative. You see, the world would like to say that there are many roads to Heaven and somehow we'll all get there eventually. But Jesus in the scripture says, **'No. There is only one.'** Just one. And that is by the road of the Cross. And God said, **'I will not meet you any other place except the Cross.'** We say, *'Now Lord, I would like to meet you some other place, on some other ground.'* God says, 'No.' Suppose I had an appointment or asked for an appointment with the President or he asked for an appointment with me and gave me the time, and I wrote back and told, *'No, that's not very convenient Mr. President. I don't think I* *can make it.'* No. I would write back and say that certainly it would be convenient. God says, **'I want an appointment with you. I want to forgive your sins. I want to change your life. I want to make you a new person.'** But God sets the conditions. And Jesus said, **'The way to Heaven is very narrow.'** Jesus was broadminded in many ways, but in other ways He was narrow. And He said, **'It is a narrow gate that leads to Heaven and the entrance to that gate is a Cross. And to the world it is an offence.'**

We don't like the Cross. But I tell you there is no alternative. It demands from every man as his first duty to get right with God. And we can talk about ritualism and works, and all the rest – and the offence of the Cross will cease. I found in my preaching I can touch on any other subject. It's popular, but not the Cross. It's an offence. It's a scandal. The world stumbles over it. And that is the very reason why thousands are not in the Kingdom of God tonight and thousands are not truly Christians tonight; because they've never been to the cross. And once you've been to the Cross and had the experience of His forgiveness and had an encounter with the Christ of the Cross you are never the same.

But I would not like to close this message tonight leaving you to think that Christ stayed on the cross. He didn't. They took Him down from the Cross. They put Him in a tomb. He stayed there three days and three nights. And on the third morning Mary, Mary Magdalene and Salome went out to get a dead body. He wasn't there. And the angel was there. And the angel gave the greatest news the world has ever heard '**He is not here; He is risen.**' And tonight I do not offer you people here a dead Christ. I offer a risen savior. A triumphant savior whose presence is here tonight. But he says, 'Before you can come to me in victory, before you can be raised, before you can have the triumph and the joy, and the crown there must first be the Cross.' And I ask you tonight, *'Have you been to the Cross?'* Are you sure of it? You say, *'Well, Billy, how do you go to the Cross?'* There are two things. One way, but there are two implications. First, you must be willing to repent of your sins. Jesus said, "Except ye repent, ye will likewise perish." You acknowledge that you are a sinner and when you come to the Cross you are acknowledging that. And you must be willing to renounce your sins that means that you change your view about God; you change your view about Christ, yourself and your neighbor; it means a change is ready to take place in your life. That change is called repentance.

And then you must be willing by faith to receive Christ as your Lord and savior, and take your stand with Him at the Cross. **But as many as received Him to them gave He power to become the children of God, even to them that believe on His name.** And do you know why many people today do not have the power to live a good life? – oh, they want to be good. They want to do the right thing, but they don't find any power within them. I'll tell you why--- They've never been to the Cross. Because when you come to the Cross and share the rejection of Christ, and share Christ at the Cross, then you become crucified with the Christ never again to live; yet, not you, but Christ lives in you and through you to give you a new power, a new dynamic and a new dimension to life – they joy and peace that He brings to the soul. He gives you that sense of fulfillment and completeness. And He can be yours tonight.

You say, 'How long will that take?' - that quick. Just like that you can receive Christ. That's only the beginning. But it does mean that you change your way of living, you change the direction of your life; you are coming to the cross; you are giving your life to Him and the Cross becomes the beginning of a new and thrilling and glorious life. And even though it's an offence--- this foolishness, this offence, this scandal of God that is called the Cross becomes gloriously planned in the mind of the Trinity; becomes the entrance to a new and glorious and thrilling existence that will last for eternity and you become a partaker of eternal life. And then you have the power to live the Christian principles and live by the sermon on the mount. He gives you a new path.

It's all yours tonight and it's free. Christ paid for it on the Cross. I'm going to ask all of you to receive Him tonight. And I want to tell you there is a danger in putting it off, because you can only come to Christ when

He speaks to you. And tonight He is speaking to many of you. And this is your moment and your night to give your life to Him, and if you don't tonight, you may never. The Bible says, **'He, that being often reproved hardeneth his neck, shall suddenly be destroyed, and that without remedy.'** Don't you presume on the mercy of God. He died for you on the Cross. He shed His blood. He loved you so much and He loved me so much that He was willing to die, but don't presume on that. I'm going to ask you to come, right now. Just get up out of your seat everywhere and stand right here. You may be a member of the church, you might not be a member of any church. And if you are a member of the church you want to come and receive Him and renew that vow that first you took. If you are not a member of any church you are coming to receive Him for the first time. You come right now, quickly.---The choir is going to sing softly, by standing here you are saying that you want to give your life to Christ; we are going to share a moment of prayer together and a verse of scripture. You may be in a delegation or with friends or relatives; they'll wait for you. You just come right now.

There are many people streaming down every aisle here, hundreds of people. There are many of you, sitting in your living room at home. You'd like to be here and come down this aisle and give your life to Christ; you can right where you are. Right now, you can say quietly inside, "Lord Jesus come in, I am a sinner and I need you. You may be in some nightclub and the television set is on, you may be in a bar, you may be in the home of a friend. Bow your head and give your life to Christ now. Then go to church tomorrow; tell your minister what you've done. Tell him you want to take your stand with Christ no matter what it costs. Get a Bible and start reading it, spend a little while in prayer each day, witness for Christ by living for Him. And God bless you.

Chapter 7 - Salvation and Forgiveness

1979 Halifax, Nova Scotia

Now tonight the 19th Chapter of Luke's Gospel beginning at verse 1. And yesterday or day before yesterday the mayor of Halifax spoke to us and he referred to this little incident that preceded the one I'm going to read to you, because Jesus is passing through Jericho at this point in scripture and a blind man screamed out and said, **'Jesus thou the son of David have mercy upon me'** and Jesus touched him. And he was healed. And now he's passing right through the middle of Jericho and another incident happens at the same time. And Jesus entered and passed through Jericho and behold there was the man named Zacchaeus which was a chief among the publicans. And he was very rich. And he sought to see Jesus who he was; and he could not for the press - that means the press of the crowd, that doesn't mean the media. Because he was little of statue and he climbed up into a sycamore tree to see Him for He was to pass that way. And when Jesus came to the place He looked up and saw him, and said to him 'Zacchaeus make haste and come down, for today I must stay at your house.'And he made haste. He came down and received Him joyfully. And when they saw it they all murmured in saying that He was gone to be the guest with the man who's a sinner. And Zacchaeus stood and said to the Lord 'Behold, Lord, the half of all my goods I give to the poor. And if I have defrauded anyone of anything, I restore it fourfold.' And Jesus said to him, 'Today salvation has come to this house, because he, too, is a son of Abraham. For the Son of Man has come to seek and to save that which was lost.' The Son of Man has come to seek and to save that which is lost.

And there are thousands of people here tonight that are lost. You are not lost from your parents so much or lost from your friends. You are lost from God. You are separated from God. And Jesus has come to seek you out and He sought out Zacchaeus. And I'll tell you the story as Jesus was passing through Jericho. You see, Zacchaeus was a publican that meant that he was a tax gatherer, he worked for Rome, he was rich, he was despised, and he was a social outcast. The people didn't like the tax gatherers – gathering taxes for a foreign country that dominated them. And if Jesus had considered public opinion, He would have never once glanced at Zacchaeus, but Jesus never considered public opinion. The scripture says, **'On all occasions Jesus made himself of no reputation.'** I imagine it had been many months since anyone crossed voluntarily into Zacchaeus' house – a man of great riches, but he was a lonely man; he was a hated man. But his curiosity got the best of him – he wanted to see Jesus. He'd possibly heard about Jesus and he'd heard them calling Him many names. Some people had called Jesus a Devil. Some said He was a fanatic. Some said He was a blasphemer. Some said He was a heretic. Some said He was a prophet. Some said He was impostor. And many said that He was actually the Son of God, so naturally Zacchaeus had a tremendous curiosity to see Jesus.

It was like when the Pope came to the United States or to Ireland, or to Poland, or to Mexico – the curiosity to see the Pope, especially an Eastern Pope. And a little boy was asked in Boston after the Pope passed by--- the television cameras came in and they put a little microphone in front of him and said, *'What did the pope look like?'- 'Well he said he had a big cowboy hat on and he was dressed in a beautiful dress.'* Well we all wanted to see the Pope or some outstanding person like that and so he wanted to see for himself.

John Calvin once said that curiosity and simplicity are a preparation to faith and how true it is. But you see to see Jesus he had some obstacles in his way: to get to Jesus. There was the press of the crowd – a big crowd. And he was a little fellow. And trying to push his way through the crowd was very difficult and he was also small of statue. He was a very small man. And to get through the crowd was almost an impossibility, because everybody wanted to get close to Jesus. And many of you would like to know Jesus and you'd like to get close to Jesus and you'd like to have Jesus in your heart, and you'd like to have salvation, but you face many obstacles. What are they? Let's just list a few that you face.

First is pride. The Bible teaches that pride keeps more people from Christ than any other sin. The sin of pride. The Bible says **'God resists the proud, but gives grace to the humble.'** The Bible says, **'If any man among you seemeth to be wise in this world, let him become a fool that he may be wise.'** Jesus said, **'We have to become as little children to be converted.'** And if you ought to get close to Christ and have Christ in your heart you may be wise, but you must become a fool. You must become as a child. You see, we are all proud. And we don't like to humble ourselves.

And then the second thing that keeps us from Christ is idolatry. And idolatry is another sin. All the way through the scriptures it is keeping more people from God then almost any other sin. And our idolatry is very unique in our day, because we worship ourselves. We worship man. Whether we realize it or not we are worshiping ourselves to things that we've created. The things we've made with our hands whether it's a television set or a new automobile – materialism. All of these things have become gods and goddesses, sex has become a goddess--- just as it was in the days of Rome. These are the modern gods. And the scripture says, **'All idolaters shall have their part in the lake which burneth with fire and brimstone: which is the second death.'** in Revelation 21:8. God hates idolatry.

And then the third thing that may keep you from Christ is worldliness. **'For what shall it profit a man, if he shall gain the whole world, and lose his own soul? Or what shall a man give in exchange for his soul'**, said Jesus in Matthew 16. There are many of you that are selling your soul, your eternal spirit for a little bit of this world. But Jesus said, 'Suppose you've had all the oil of the Middle East, all the gold of South Africa, all the diamonds, the wealth of the whole world--- and you had it all, all the music, all the culture, all the philosophy, all the psychology of the world--- you had it all and lost your soul. It wouldn't be worth it. And yet you are losing your soul for just a little bit of it. Not that that doesn't mean that you are not to have money. Nowhere in the Bible does God condemn a wealthy man unless he misuses it or unless he got it the wrong way. Then he's condemned. But the Bible says, ' **know ye not that the friendship with the world is enmity with God? whosoever therefore will be a friend of the world is the enemy of God.'** Now what does that word 'world' mean? It's cosmos. It means a world's system dominated by evil. That evil part of the world system in which we live. Friendship with that means enmity with God. And God says, **'Wherefore come out from among them, and be ye separate, saith the Lord, and touch not the unclean thing.'**

World in the New Testament meant a relationship that people had with their social environment; we are to be separated from the evils of the world. Now perhaps you saw those pictures on television a few months ago of some 40 whales who for some unknown biological reason beached themselves and died. They left their living environment and died. And many of you have left the environment of living in the scriptures and living for God and gone out into the world, and your soul is dead toward God. You deliberately bring on your own spiritual death; you promote your own internal death by going with the evils of the world round about you. And the world round about you squeezes you into its mold. The Bible says that you are going to give up the wrong things in the world: the lust and the greed, and the hate, and the prejudice, and the materialism – part of the world that's wrong--- you have to turn from, when you come to Christ. And that's the reason why it is so hard to follow Christ in the modern day. It's not easy to be a Christian. I'm not going to fool you. I would think it's more difficult to be a Christian right now in modern America or modern western world than any other part of the world.

You see to be a Christian in some parts of the Orient or some other parts of the world you have to really stand for Christ, and you have to suffer. But in a country where there is no suffering and no physical prosecution it's rather easy just to slide along really not knowing Christ--- calling yourself a Christian, but not really being a Christian, not a New Testament Christian. And there are thousands of people like that who have gone to church all their lives and been baptized, and confirmed, but still not knowing Christ.

And then another obstacle – the secret sins, the Bible says, the psalmist prayed, **'Cleanse thou me from secret faults.'**The Bible says, **'for Thou hast set our iniquities before thee, our secret sins in the light of thy countenance. For God shall bring every work into judgment, with every secret thing,...'** And Paul wrote to the Romans **' the day when God shall judge the secrets of men by Jesus Christ according to my gospel.'**

You can keep no secrets from God. You may sweep some of the dirt under the rug, but God will find it. It's there. All of His tapes have been running--- not only of your actions and your words, but your thoughts, your intents, all the moral choices you could have made are all there in His computers. So that at the Day of Judgment you will try to open your mouth to defend yourself, but there will be no defense. Your secret sins--- and you know what they are. Your friends don't know anything about them. You family might not even know, but you know. And God has been speaking to you about them. It's like the Incredible Hulk on television. I think I've seen it once, maybe twice. But I've read about it. And if I understand it correctly, it's trying to get rid of the person inside of him always. And perhaps you've been battling with the hidden man in your heart with your secret sins.

Confess them to Christ tonight. Come to the Cross and bring those secrets of your heart and lay them before Him and say, *'Lord, here they are. I surrender.'*

And then self-righteousness is another thing that keeps people form Christ. **There is a generation,** the

Bible says, **that are pure in their own eyes and yet they have not been washed from their filthiness.** Pure in our own eyes. Saying we are good, when actually we are bad; saying we are good, when actually we are sinning and breaking God's laws. That keeps us from Christ – self-righteousness.

Now we've seen the obstacles, let's look at Jesus. It's a personal call: Jesus turns to Zacchaeus and calls him by name. He sees Zacchaeus up the tree, you see Zacchaeus had climbed the sycamore tree and him sitting there watching Jesus, and all of a sudden the most unpopular man in town, the most hated man in town, the most sinful man in town, and here's his name called by the great prophet Jesus. And Jesus says, **'Zacchaeus!'** Can you imagine how startled he was that out of all the crowd and those religious leaders he the worst sinner in town called by his name. The Bible says, **'Jesus is a good shepherd. He calls his own sheep by name and leads them out.'**

In Genesis we read that God came to the Garden of Eden personally to call Adam. He said, **'Adam, where art thou?'** And later He called Abraham. He said, **'Abraham--- Jacob--- Moses---Joshua--- Gideon -- Samuel--- David---Solomon---'** He called them all by name. --- **Isaiah--- Jeremiah--- Ezekiel--- Daniel**--- He called them by name. And then when the Lord Jesus Christ came He called His disciples by name. He went down to the seashore and He called out **Simon and Peter--- Andrew--- James--- John---** And from the receipt of custom another man like Zacchaeus, a tax gatherer--- **Matthew come and follow me.** And he rose and followed Jesus immediately.

And on the Damascus road he said, **'Saul, Saul, why do you persecute me?'** On the isle of Patmos--- **John---** He called you by name. What is your name? Jim, Suzy, Peter? He called you by name tonight. He knows your name. He knows all about you. And he called you. And He says, *'Mary, get out of your seat and come and receive Me tonight. I want to come into your house and* into your heart.' 'Jim, you need Me. You know you need Me to help you, to forgive you, to take you to Heaven. Get out of your seat and come.'

He called you by name. He looked up in the trees and said, **'Zacchaeus!'** And it was an urgent call. He said, **'Zacchaeus make haste. Hurry. We don't have long.'** And that's what He says to you, *'Hurry! Make haste. If you are going to come to Christ, come now. You may never have another moment like this.'* Nowhere does the Bible promise tomorrow you can be saved. It's today. Today is the day of salvation. **Now** is the accepted time. There might not be a tomorrow for you. There is a little verse in your national anthem that sometimes I miss when I hear it sung and it's a beautiful thing:

O Lord, our God, arise,

On Thee our hopes we fix,

God save us all.

Tonight that would be my prayer for you; God save us all.

The Lord came to seek and to save that which is lost. Today He's urgently calling you by name. And it was a successful call, because Zacchaeus did make haste. You know what he did? He didn't wait to climb down the tree, he jumped. And D.L. Moody, the evangelist from the century said Zaccheus was converted from the limb to the ground and I guess that was true.

The rich young ruler came to Jesus. He felt down before Jesus. He was running to Jesus, making haste to get to Jesus and he got to Jesus, but he couldn't pay the price. And he was lost. Even though Jesus loved him and Jesus tried, and Jesus talked with him, and gave him precious time. Yet, that young man never came to Jesus. But Zacchaeus, a great sinner, did come to Jesus. And Jesus went to Zacchaeus' home and I think that Jesus probably took Matthew with him. And I expect Matthew and Zacchaeus got into a conversation late into the night. And Matthew told him about his own experience.

How he'd also been a tax gatherer and how he'd been a sinner, and how Jesus had called him by name and he said, **'Follow me.'** And Matthew said, *'I got up right then and followed Him, and I've never regretted one minute of it. He changed my life. He's given me assurance. He's blessed my family. He's brought our family together. Oh, I'd die for Him. I've given Him my life.'*

And Zacchaeus heard that. And I imagine that Matthew told him that night, *'You know, Zacchaeus, if you come to Christ, if you come to Jesus, you are going to have to make some restitution, you are going to have to change your whole way of living. And you are going to have to declare openly your allegiance for Jesus Christ.'* We are to be in the world but not of it. We live in two worlds: we live in this world, but we are also citizens of another world – the Kingdom of Heaven. And our first allegiance is always to the Kingdom of Heaven.

Yes, I imagine Matthew told him all of those things. What was the result? The result was that Zacchaeus received Christ. Now receiving Christ involves an active faith beyond mere human reason. The Bible says, **'But the natural man receiveth not the things of the Spirit of God: for they are foolishness unto him: neither can he know them, because they are spiritually discerned.'** In other words, a natural person like you just cannot come and reason his way to the Kingdom of God, you cannot reason your way to Christ. I don't imagine Zacchaeus sat down and went through all of the philosophy and all the theological debates about Jesus. He just joyfully received Him, by faith. Simply like a little child. And Jesus received him and forgave him.

You see, Christ is knocking on our heart's door tonight. He's asking people like you to receive Him. And they accused Him by saying, **'This man receiveth sinners.'** Are you a sinner? Have you broken God's law? I'm a sinner. Are you? Sure you are. He receiveth sinners. Isn't that a wonderful thing that He receiveth sinners?

And if they should ask me at the gates of Heaven, when I die, *'what is the password?'* I'm going to say, *I'm here by the grace and the mercy of God, because of what*

Jesus Christ did on the Cross. I'm not going to Heaven

because I've preached in a big stadium full of people like

this tonight. I'm not going to Haven because I've read

the Bible. I'm not going to Heaven because I've prayed.

I'm not going to Heaven because of a wonderful

Christian wife and five Christian children. I'm going to

Heaven because of the grace and the mercy of God. I'm a

sinner. I deserve judgement. I deserve hell. I'm going

because of Christ. And I have received Christ. I've let Him

come into my heart. And I've come to the Cross. He's

forgiven my sin. I have eternal life. I know I'm saved

tonight. I know where I've come from. I know why I'm

here. I know where I'm going. And if he should come

tonight, I'm ready.

Do you know that? - are you sure about that? This
man receiveth sinners. But as many as received Him--- to
them gave He the power to become the sons of God
even to them that believe on His Name. And notice that

He did it joyfully. There seems to be little joy in too many of our modern lives today.

Maclean's magazine a few weeks ago had a cover story on young suicides and it said that the greatest killer in this nation is suicide. And I read the other day that even though the suicide rate in America is extremely high, yet in the Soviet Union it's even double that of the United States. So it's a worldwide phenomenon that we are seeing especially among young people. The number one killer at the universities in the United States at the moment is not heart disease, is not cancer, is not accidents but suicide. Why would a young person do that? You know why? Emptiness--- Emptiness, alienation, fear of failure--- and so they decide to end it all.

But they don't end it all. You see, you can't kill yourself. You only kill the body. Your soul, the spirit, the part of you made in the image of God is going to live forever and ever, and ever. And so all you do is just transfer to another part of life in which you are still separated from God, still alienated. But it's too late to do anything about it. The mercy of God is extended now. Here. In this life. You receive Him and let Him come into your life and you'll find what it means to be joyful.

You know, when the BeeGee's where in Canada, it was stated that their Saturday Night Fever had sold over 25 million albums. I think that's a record breaker. I'm not sure that Elvis Presley ever sold that many. But anyway, it was quoted in the paper that Barry Gibb when he smiled into the camera and looked like he was having a wonderful time made a statement that he felt inside like warmed over death. And you know, I meet a lot of these stars as we travel about. Our whole team does. All over the world we've met them. And we've found how miserable you can be at the top of the heap.

And everybody looking at you saying, *'I'd like to be like that.'* But so miserable inside. Or a person that seeks political power and he gets to the top, and he becomes maybe the President of the United States. And he thought to himself when he was a little boy, *'Or if I could only be the President of the United States, I'd be the happiest man in the world.'* And he gets in that White House and he becomes so lonely, and the burden is so great. You can almost see the President age on television. Without Christ you feel that emptiness in your life--- nothing else satisfies: sex doesn't do it, drugs don't do it, power, popularity – all of that is nothing. Christ is everything.

And then when you have Christ you are ready to live here and now, life with a capital 'L' when you really know Christ is your saviour. Yes, Zacchaeus received Christ joyfully.

I was reading in Ann Landers a while ago; I want to quote a passage by a young girl that I've read some time ago--- *Can I say something to that kid who thought pot was the greatest. I'm 18 and I've been on a terrific high for the last three years. But it's not pot that does it for me. It's Jesus. I don't need drugs or booze, my kicks come from loving Him and knowing that He loves me. And it's the greatest trip there is.* Give your life to Christ and have the greatest joy you've ever known.

And notice another thing Zacchaeus openly confessed Christ publicly. He stood in front of all of his friends in the whole town. And he said, *'I've been wrong. I've been a sinner. I'm ready to restore everything that I ever did if it's necessary. Whatever it takes. From now on I'm following Jesus Christ. He is my Lord and He is my savior. He came to seek and to save me in this town of Jericho.'* He came to Halifax in the form of this crusade to seek and to save you. And He calls you by name. And He says, 'Make haste. Come while there's time.' Because you see, the scripture says, **'Whosoever denieth the Son, the same hath not the Father. He that acknowledgeth the Son hath the Father also.'** Also the scripture says, **'Whosoever shall confess that Jesus is the Son of God, God dwelleth in him, and he in God.'** And Jesus said, **'But whoever denies Me before men, him I will also deny before My Father who is in heaven.'**

You see, Jesus Christ hung on the Cross publicly in front of hundreds of people: dying, bleeding for you. And He asks you to publicly receive Him. And I'm going to ask you to do that in a moment.

There are three things you have to do. First, listen to this so you will not stand at the Judgement Day saying, 'I never knew.'--- First, you must repent of your sin. How do you repent? The word 'repent' means to change your mind. It means to turn. You are going in this direction in your life, you turn around and start in a new direction. Now you may not be able to turn by yourself, in fact, you can't. You have to say, *'Lord, help me to turn. Help me to repent.'* That means that you are willing to let Christ come into your life to help you change your whole pattern of living, your lifestyle, everything if necessary.

And then the second thing, by faith you receive Him. Now that word faith may cause you to stumble. It means that you commit, you surrender your total life to Jesus Christ. You are not trusting any other God. You are not trusting any other religion. You are not trusting anything, but Jesus Christ and Him alone to save you. That's faith – total commitment to Christ.

And then thirdly, you are willing to follow Him, you are willing to be His disciple. Now the word disciple means learner or discipline. It means discipline, learning. You are following Him, growing in the grace and knowledge of Christ by studying the Bible, by prayer, by witnessing, by attending the church. You say, *'Billy, you know, most of those things I'm already doing.'* But do you really know Christ? Are you sure of it? If you are not sure, if you are not certain that Christ is in your heart tonight and that your sin is forgiven, He's calling you by name, He sees you and He says, *'Make haste and come.'*

I'm going to ask you to get up out of your seat right now and come and stand and say by coming, 'I want to come to the cross by faith tonight, I want to have my sins forgiven, I want to know that I have eternal life, I want to know that I'm going to heaven. You come and stand here tonight and we'll have a word of prayer together.

Afterword

Thank you for choosing this book; I pray it has been a blessing to you. Please send a gift copy to a friend or loved one; by doing so, you may be effecting a change that will have lasting eternal consequences. You may also be interested to get a copy of the bestselling:

Is Heaven for Real? Personal Stories of Visiting Heaven

http://www.amazon.com/dp/B00BXKG41U

A man is living his live as an atheist until a diving accident leaves him stone cold dead and placed in a morgue. He somehow regains consciousness, freaking out the hospital staff! Upon his return to life he tells of his journey to heaven and back.

A devoted elderly man tells of his frequent trips to heaven and the visions of Angels who guide him there.

A pastor gets hit head on by a tractor trailer and is instantly transported to heaven.

A believer on the edge of eternity tells of his vision from his hospital room.

These stories will strengthen your faith in a powerful way! Share with friends – a great witnessing tool to lead others to Christ!

If you sent a gift copy of this book to just a few friends; what an impact that could make on someone's life for eternity? What blessed hope could take root and grow! There are people you can reach that no one else can. Please share this treasure with others; here is the link for you:

http://www.amazon.com/dp/1483915263

and the second volume:

http://www.amazon.com/dp/1484988299

IS HEAV...
FOR REA...

2

Personal Stories
of
Visiting Heaven

Patrick Doucette

Appendix – A list of all past Billy Graham Crusade Locations by date and city

Did you ever attend a Billy Graham Crusade? Perhaps you did but can't remember when or where it was. Here is a list of the locations where Billy Graham conducting stadium preaching events in chronological order from 1947 to 2005.

1947
Grand Rapids, Michigan
Charlotte, North Carolina

1948
Augusta, Georgia
Modesto, California

1949
Miami, Florida
Baltimore, Maryland
Altoona, Pennsylvania
Los Angeles, California

1950
Boston, Massachusetts
Columbia, South Carolina
Tour-New England States
Portland, Oregon
Minneapolis, Minnesota

Atlanta, Georgia
1951
Tour-Southern States
Fort Worth, Texas
Shreveport, Louisiana
Cincinnati, Ohio
Memphis, Tennessee
Seattle, Washington
Hollywood, California
Greensboro, North Carolina
Raleigh, North Carolina

1952
Washington, District of Columbia
Houston, Texas
Jackson, Mississippi
Pittsburgh, Pennsylvania
Albuquerque, New Mexico

1953
Tour-Florida Cities
Chattanooga, Tennessee
St. Louis, Missouri
Dallas, Texas
Tour-West Texas
Syracuse, New York
Detroit, Michigan
Asheville, North Carolina

1954
London, England
Tour-Europe/Amsterdam, Berlin,
Copenhagen, Dusseldorf, Frankfurt,
Helsinki, Paris, Stockholm
Nashville, Tennessee
New Orleans, Louisiana

Tour-West Coast

1955
Glasgow, Scotland
Tour-Scotland Cities
London, England
Paris, France
Zurich, Switzerland
Geneva, Switzerland
Mannheim, West Germany
Stuttgart, West Germany
Nurnberg, West Germany
Dortmund, West Germany
Frankfurt, West Germany
Tour U.S. Service Bases, West Germany
Rotterdam, The Netherlands
Oslo, Norway
Gothenburg, Sweden
Aarhus, Denmark
Toronto, Ontario, Canada

1956
Tour-India and Far East
Richmond, Virginia
Oklahoma City, Oklahoma
Louisville, Kentucky

1957
New York, New York

1958
Tour-Caribbean
San Francisco, California
Sacramento, California
Fresno, California
Santa Barbara, California

Los Angeles, California
San Diego, California
San Antonio, Texas
Charlotte, North Carolina

1959
Melbourne, Australia
Auckland, New Zealand
Sydney, Australia
Perth, Australia
Brisbane, Australia
Adelaide, Australia
Wellington, New Zealand
Christchurch, New Zealand
Canberra, Launceston and
Hobart, Australia
Little Rock, Arkansas
Wheaton, Illinois
Indianapolis, Indiana

1960
Monrovia, Liberia
Accra, Ghana
Kumasi, Ghana
Lagos, Nigeria
Ibadan, Nigeria
Kaduna, Nigeria
Enugu, Nigeria
Jos, Nigeria
Brazzaville, Congo
Bulawayo, South Rhodesia
Salisbury, Rhodesia
Kitwe, North Rhodesia
Moshi, Tanganyika
Kisumu, Kenya
Usumbura, Ruanda-Urundi

Nairobi, Kenya
Addis Ababa, Ethiopia
Cairo, Egypt
Jerusalem, Jordan
Washington, District of Columbia
Rio de Janeiro, Brazil
Bern, Switzerland
Zurich, Switzerland
Basel, Switzerland
Lausanne, Switzerland
Essen, West Germany
Hamburg, West Germany
Berlin, West Germany
New York, (Spanish), New York

1961
Jacksonville, Florida
Orlando, Florida
Clearwater, Florida
St. Petersburg, Florida
Tampa, Florida
Bradenton-Sarasota, Florida
Tallahassee, Florida
Gainesville, Florida
Miami, Florida
Cape Canaveral, Florida
West Palm Beach, Florida
Vero Beach, Florida
Peace River, Florida
Boca Raton, Florida
Fort Lauderdale, Florida
Manchester, England
Glasgow, Scotland
Belfast, Ireland
Minneapolis/St. Paul, Minnesota
Philadelphia, Pennsylvania

1962
Tour-South America
Raleigh, North Carolina
Jacksonville, North Carolina
Chicago, Illinois
Seattle, Washington
Fresno, California
Redstone Arsenal, Alabama
Tour-South America
El Paso, Texas

1963
Paris, France
Lyon, France
Toulouse, France
Mulhouse, France
Montauban, France
Nancy, France
Douai, France
Nurnberg, West Germany
Stuttgart, West Germany
Los Angeles, California

1964
Birmingham, Alabama
Phoenix, Arizona
San Diego, California
Columbus, Ohio
Omaha, Nebraska
Boston, Massachusetts (Sept)
Boston, Massachusetts (Oct)
Manchester, New Hampshire
Portland, Maine
Bangor, Maine
Providence, Rhode Island

Louisville, Kentucky

1965
Honolulu, Oahu, Hawaii
Kahului, Maui, Hawaii
Hilo, Hawaii,
Lihue, Kauai, Hawaii
Dothan, Alabama
Tuscaloosa, Alabama (U. of Alabama)
Auburn University, Alabama
Tuskegee Institute, Alabama
Montgomery, Alabama
Copenhagen, Denmark
Vancouver, British Columbia, Canada
Seattle, Washington
Denver, Colorado
Houston, Texas

1966
Greenville, South Carolina
London, England
Berlin, West Germany

1967
Ponce, Puerto Rico
San Juan, Puerto Rico
Winnipeg, Manitoba, Canada
London, England
Turin, Italy
Zagreb, Yugoslavia
Toronto, Ontario, Canada
Kansas City, Missouri
Tokyo, Japan

1968
Brisbane, Australia

Sydney, Australia
Portland, Oregon
San Antonio, Texas
Pittsburgh, Pennsylvania

1969
Auckland, New Zealand
Dunedin, New Zealand
Melbourne, Australia
New York, New York
Anaheim, California

1970
Dortmund, West Germany
Knoxville, Tennessee
New York, New York
Baton Rouge, Louisiana

1971
Lexington, Kentucky
Chicago, Illinois
Oakland, California
Dallas/Fort Worth, Texas

1972
Charlotte, North Carolina
Birmingham, Alabama
Cleveland, Ohio
Kohima, Nagaland, India

1973
Durban, South Africa
Johannesburg, South Africa
Seoul, Korea (South)
Atlanta, Georgia
Minneapolis/St. Paul, Minnesota

Raleigh, North Carolina
St. Louis, Missouri

1974
Phoenix, Arizona
Los Angeles, California
 (25th Anniversary Celebration)
Rio de Janeiro, Brazil
Norfolk/Hampton, Virginia

1975
Albuquerque, New Mexico
Jackson, Mississippi
Brussels, Belgium
Lubbock, Texas
Taipei, Taiwan
Hong Kong

1976
Seattle, Washington
Williamsburg, Virginia
San Diego, California
Detroit, Michigan
Nairobi, Kenya

1977
Gothenburg, Sweden
Asheville, North Carolina
South Bend, Indiana
Tour Hungary
Cincinnati, Ohio
Manila, Philippines
India-Good News Festivals

1978
Las Vegas, Nevada

Memphis, Tennessee
Toronto, Ontario, Canada
Kansas City, Missouri
Oslo, Norway
Stockholm, Sweden
Satellite Locations in Sweden
Satellite Locations in Norway
Satellite Locations In Iceland
Tour Poland
Singapore

1979
Sao Paulo, Brazil
Tampa, Florida
Sydney, Australia
Nashville, Tennessee
1979 cont'd
Milwaukee, Wisconsin
Halifax, Nova Scotia, Canada

1980
Oxford, England
Cambridge, England
Indianapolis, Indiana
Edmonton, Alberta, Canada
Wheaton, Illinois
Okinawa, Japan
Osaka, Japan
Fukuoka, Japan
Tokyo, Japan
Reno, Nevada
Las Vegas, Nevada

1981
Mexico City, Mexico
Villahermosa, Mexico

Boca Raton, Florida
Baltimore, Maryland
Calgary, Alberta, Canada
San Jose, California
Houston, Texas

1982
Blackpool, England
Providence, Rhode Island
Burlington, Vermont
Portland, Maine
Springfield, Massachusetts
Manchester, New Hampshire
Moscow, Russia
Hartford, Connecticut
New Haven, Connecticut
Boston, Massachusetts
 (Northeastern University)
Amherst, Massachusetts
 (University of Massachusetts)
New Haven, Connecticut
 (Yale University)
Cambridge, Massachusetts
 (Harvard University)
Newton, Massachusetts
 (Boston College)
Cambridge, Massachusetts
 (Massachusetts Institute of Technology)
South Hamilton, Massachusetts
 (Gordon-Conwell Seminary)
Hanover, New Hampshire
 (Dartmouth College)
Boston, Massachusetts
New Orleans, Louisiana
 (Southern Baptist Convention
 Evangelistic Rally)

Boise, Idaho
Spokane, Washington
Chapel Hill, North Carolina
German Democratic Republic
 Wittenberg
 Dresden (Saxony)
 Gorlitz
 Stendal
 Stralsund
 Berlin
Czechoslovakia
 Prague
 Brno
 Bratislava
Nassau, Bahamas

1983
Orlando, Florida
Tacoma, Washington
Sacramento, California
Oklahoma City, Oklahoma

1984
Anchorage, Alaska
Mission England
 Bristol, England
 Sunderland, England
 Norwich, England
 Birmingham, England
 Liverpool, England
 Ipswich, England
Seoul, Korea (South)
Union of Soviet Socialist Republics
 Leningrad, Russia
 Tallinn, Estonia
 Novosibirsk, Siberia

Moscow, Russia
Vancouver, British Columbia, Canada

1985
Fort Lauderdale, Florida
Hartford, Connecticut
Sheffield, England
Anaheim, California
Romania
 Suceava
 Cluj-Napoca
 Oradea
 Arad
 Timisoara
 Sibiu
 Bucharest
Hungary
 Pecs
 Budapest

1986
Washington, D.C.
Paris, France
Tallahassee, Florida

1987
Columbia, South Carolina
Cheyenne, Wyoming
Fargo, North Dakota
Billings, Montana
Sioux Falls, South Dakota
Denver, Colorado
Helsinki, Finland

1988
People's Republic of China

Beijing
Huaiyin
Nanjing
Shanghai
Guangzhou
Union of Soviet Socialist Republics
Zagorsk, Russia
Moscow, Russia
Kiev, Ukraine
Buffalo, New York
Rochester, New York
Hamilton, Ontario, Canada

1989
Syracuse, New York
London, England
Budapest, Hungary
Little Rock, Arkansas

1990
Berlin, West Germany
Montreal, Quebec, Canada
Albany, New York
Uniondale (Long Island), New York˙
Hong Kong

1991
Seattle and Tacoma, Washington
Scotland
Edinburgh
Aberdeen
Glasgow
East Rutherford, New Jersey
New York, New York (Central Park)
Buenos Aires, Argentina

1992
Pyongyang, Korea (North)
Philadelphia, Pennsylvania
Portland, Oregon
Moscow, Russia

1993
Essen, Germany
Pittsburgh, Pennsylvania
Columbus, Ohio

1994
Tokyo, Japan
Beijing, People's Republic of China
Pyongyang, Korea (North)
Cleveland, Ohio
Atlanta, Georgia

1995
San Juan, Puerto Rico
Global Mission
Toronto, Ontario, Canada
Sacramento, California

1996
World Television Series
Minneapolis/St. Paul, Minnesota
Charlotte, North Carolina

1997
San Antonio, Texas
San Jose, California
San Francisco, California
Oakland, California

1998

Ottawa, Ontario, Canada
Tampa, Florida

1999
Indianapolis, Indiana
St. Louis, Missouri

2000
Nashville, Tennessee
Jacksonville, Florida

2001
Louisville, Kentucky
Fresno, California

2002
Cincinnati, Ohio
Dallas/Fort Worth, Texas

2003
San Diego, California
Oklahoma City, Oklahoma

2004
Kansas City, Missouri
Los Angeles, California

2005
New York, New York